MW01487703

famished

MARYMOUNT
INSTITUTE PRESS

Famished: A Food Memoir with Recipes
Copyright © 2018 by Heather King. All rights reserved.

Apart from any fair dealing for the purpose of private study, research, criticism or review, as permitted under the Copyright Act, no part of this publication may be reproduced in any form, stored in a retrieval system or transmitted in any form by any means—electronic, mechanical, photocopy, recording or otherwise—without the prior permission of the publisher. Enquiries should be sent to the address mentioned below.

TSEHAI and Marymount Institute Press books may be purchased for educational, business, or sales promotional use. For more information, please contact our special sales department.

Marymount Institute Press
an imprint of TSEHAI Publishers
Loyola Marymount University
1 LMU Drive, UH 3012, Los Angeles, CA 90045

www.tsehaipublishers.com/mip
mip@tsehaipublishers.com

Paperback ISBN: 978-1-941392-14-0

First Edition: 2018

Publisher: Elias Wondimu
Typesetting and Cover Design: Sara Martinez
Copyediting: Theresia de Vroom & Jeff Nazzaro
Editorial Assistant: Elizabeth Rahe
Photographs by: Madeline Wilson

A catalog record data for this book is available from:
U.S. Library of Congress, Washington, DC, USA
British Library, London, UK
Wemezekir Ethiopian National Library, Addis Ababa, Ethiopia

10 9 8 7 6 5 4 3 2 1

Printed in the United States of America

Los Angeles | Addis Ababa | Oxford | Johannesburg

Acknowledgments

I'd like first to thank Jeff Dietrich: I rode the coattails of his own book for the Marymount Institute Press and TSEHAI Publishers: *The Good Samaritan: Stories from the Los Angeles Catholic Worker on Skid Row.*

If Jeff hadn't invited me to his book launch, I would never have met editor extraordinaire Theresia de Vroom. If I hadn't met Theresia, I wouldn't have met exiled Ethiopian journalist and publisher Elias Wondimu, the brains and heart behind TSEHAI Publishers. And if all three of those people hadn't, out of their own Good Samaritan spirits, supported my life and work, *Famished* might never have seen the light of day.

Thanks as well to photographer Madeline Wilson, who came with Theresia to my apartment and snapped away: Theresia expertly oversaw, and Madeline expertly and creatively photographed, the making of several of the recipes. Special thanks to the wondrous Sara Martinez for her extraordinary design and Jeff Nazzaro for his painstaking copyediting skills.

Finally, my undying gratitude to the many people who have offered me their homes, vacation homes, beach homes, and guest rooms in which to stay and work for various periods of time. They, too, are Good Samaritans of the first order, and include Christine Madsen, Julia Gibson and Aaron Lipstadt, Father Patrick Dooling, and Father Tom Hall.

Introduction

We dream about food, plan around food, live for and by food.

We have books about cooking food. We have books about growing food. We have books about nutrition, local sourcing, and becoming a celebrity chef. We have Michael Pollan, guru of the "real food" movement, dispensing earnest rules.

But we have few books about the spiritual dimension of food that *also have a sense of humor*. We have few books exploring the way our relationship to—and neuroses around—food shape our relationships to money, sex, love, and the search for meaning.

Famished treats the Eucharistic overtones of food: food as an echo of our longing for transcendence and communion; food as a manifestation of our fears, our obsessive compulsions, our quirks; food—ordinary, everyday food—as a sacrament, a mystery, and a source of unending reflection and delight.

In this collection loosely related, loosely narrative essays, I tell my story—one of eight kids in a blue-collar family in which the overriding emotion was financial anxiety; twenty years of hard-core drinking; a move from Boston to LA; a marriage that bore fruit but didn't last; the lawyering job I quit to embark on the perilous vocation of writing; my conversion to Catholicism; cancer; divorce; cross-country road trips.

Through the essays runs the story of my love affair with food: foraged food, street food, my tendency to hoard food, the occasional all-out dinner parties I throw, the splendor of cooking, the shared meal as perhaps the highest form of human communion.

I write of the unfolding discovery that the human condition is not a sickness to be healed but a paradox to be pondered, patiently endured, and

ecstatically, abundantly, lived.

I've included recipes, as did M. F. K. Fisher, Ruth Reichl, A. J. Liebling, and many others who have written "literary" food memoirs. Robert Farrar Capon (*The Supper of the Lamb*), for one, wrote beautifully of God and food.

I'm honored to follow in their footsteps and I also hope that my own take is unique and new. As editor Theresia de Vroom observes, "Eighty percent of the paintings you see of Christ are of the Madonna and Child. Not the Baptism, not the Temptation in the Desert, not the Resurrection. In our most iconic image of Christ, he's in Mary's lap, drinking milk from her breast."

In turn, we allow ourselves to be consumed: by love—so that others may eat.

≥ 1 ≤

Our Holy Hunger

Oh! Those who don't believe in the sun ... are real infidels! The sun, light in the darkness, light that brightens nature and people, light that calls the dead from their graves. Those who have eyes to see will recognize that all light comes from the same sun."

—Vincent van Gogh, *Letters to Theo*

I've always been drawn to books about people in mental institutions, prisons, death camps: Genie, the feral child who, after rescue, would hoard up to fifteen glasses of water by her bed; Shin Dong-hyuk, the only known person to have been born in a North Korean starvation camp, escaped and survived; Marthe Robin, the French "holy anorexic," who reputedly subsisted for decades on the Host alone (and no sleep).

I grew up on the coast of New Hampshire, one of eight kids. My father, a bricklayer, and my mother, a housewife, both came from want of various kinds. Dad's version of their financial backstory ran, "We started out with twenty-five dollars and Mother's sewing machine." They were married by a justice of the peace (weddings cost). My father spoke, often, of a place called "the poorhouse."

We had everything we needed—books, a piano, a love of nature—but emotionally and financially, a sense of scarcity reigned. Having as few needs, and taking up as little room, as possible seemed a sane psychic strategy to ward off the angst. That worked—up to a point. Then, in my case, the

angst segued into self-deprivation, neurotic guilt and codependence. Even today, against the threat of abandonment, I have no psychic cartilage, no cushion: just bone scraping against bone; flooding pain. I've never been able to bear wasting food. Even today, I have a tendency to hoard food.

That in my early forties I converted to Catholicism is no accident. A God who, out of love, took on our humanity, pitched his tent among us, and left us his very Body to eat and Blood to drink is my kind of God. "[Jesus] did not need anyone to testify about human nature. He himself understood it well" [John 2:25]. He understood our terrible hunger: for connection, for love, to know we're not alone. He understood what we will do to each other when our hungers are unfulfilled.

We ate what was put in front of us in my house and we were grateful for it. We rarely went to the doctor as kids: that, too, has shaped me. I love food but I'm not fussy about it. *Eat what you want and take a walk* is my theory. I don't own a pair of bathroom scales and weigh pretty much the same as I did in high school. Nonfat anything depresses me. I adore gluten. I'm almost never sick. At sixty-five, I take no medications. I rarely, and don't really know how to, cook meat—not because meat is bad for me or to make a political statement, but because for much of my life I haven't been much able to *afford* meat.

On the other hand, when a friend sent me half a dozen Royal Riviera pears last Christmas, I was touched to the core. Another friend, who owns twelve houses, a car, a pickup truck, a motorcycle, and an advertising business happened to see the shipping charges on the Harry and David box and sniffed at "the extravagance." She was confusing shrewd business practices with generosity of spirit, as Judas did before betraying Christ. She mentioned the people in "sub-Saharan Africa," but what she really meant was: "You and your friends will never get ahead if you exchange such profligate gifts." With all her possessions, she was poor, and she was blind. I gave five of the pears away—including one to her—and kept the sixth, nestled in grass-green tissue paper, gold foil, and a fluted white nest, to savor for myself.

For much of the writing of this book, I lived in the hipster LA neighborhood of Silver Lake. I've since moved to Pasadena, but wherever I live, I am in the world, but not quite of it. My days are monk-like: prayer, writing, answering emails, cleaning my room, walking to Mass, pondering.

And always and forever, eating. Food: the sacrament in which we are made to partake three times a day! Hunger: the incarnate reality and the inexhaustible metaphor.

"We are conscious of the insufficiency and inadequacy of our explanations," observed John Paul II. That hardly have we eaten before we're hungry again is its own kind of insufficiency. Then again, how God must love us to want to be so ceaselessly and so often near!

The world tells us to tamp down our hungers—to become health-conscious, effective, and neat. Christ says go for broke. Christ says make a fool of yourself, wear your heart on your sleeve, be a pest. Eat with your fingers, wipe your hands on your pants, let juice run down your chin. Climb up the sycamore tree and wave your arms. Throw yourself on the ground and give thanks. Set out on a long journey without knowing the destination.

Weep for the hungry, the war-torn, the poor. Order your life around them. Our hungers are our ticket to paradise. Our wounds make us more useful, more compassionate, and more complex than we could ever be sanitized and scarless.

That childhood anxiety, for example, has given me a capacity for joy and the ability to wonder at, and give thanks for, "small things." I collect seed pods, stones, leaves from the sidewalk. I keep cards that people have sent me, sometimes for years. When you never expect things to go right and they do, you're brought to your knees with gratitude. I have wept at times over indoor plumbing, sheets on my bed, toothpaste, the sun!

Driving cross-country several years ago, I stopped at the CVS in Watsontown, Pennsylvania, to buy a pint of half-and-half for my morning coffee, feeling an insane amount of pleasure because I'd remembered to bring a clothespin with which to clamp the carton shut and therefore have cream for a day or two. As the Italian poet Cesare Pavese (1908–50) observed: "Religion consists of the belief that *everything that happens to us is extraordinarily important*. It can never disappear from the world for this reason." One of the fruits of thinking that everything's important is that you begin to live every second in such a way that all your powers and talents and faculties are brought to a sort of thrilling, vitalized, height. Either that, or like Pavese, you kill yourself.

Was Christ "happy"? I sometimes wonder. Nietzsche said that Christ never laughed, but I refuse to believe that the Son of Man didn't crack up at a good, black- humor joke.

As a single, childless creative writer in Los Angeles (as opposed to TV and film writers, who apparently actually make money), I *have* to have a sense of humor. In fact, one of my heroes is LA writer Sandra Tsing Loh's

elderly father, who, with a masters in physics and a PhD in mechanical engineering, apparently used to go around a Malibu Starbucks nabbing left-behind half-drunk lattes, grande drips, and mochachinos that he downed while reading an *LA Times* fished from the trash bin.

I thoroughly approve. I think he hitchhiked, too, and I look ever forward to *truly* old age, when you can be any damn kind of kook you want.

RUSSIAN BLACK BREAD

Makes 2 loaves

I'm a mid-grade cook: not super-accomplished, but able to make most things by following a recipe. I'm going to assume the same is true for you.

Bread—the staff of life—is so not hard to make. (What *is* hard to make, for me, is pie crust, but that's another story). Bread is flour, yeast, kneading with your hands, and the best smell in the world. You really can't go wrong. So go out on a limb. Give it a try. The worst that can happen is the bread doesn't rise properly, in which case you have hardtack and can be in solidarity with the pioneers who explored the western frontier.

Deb Perelman of Smitten Kitchen—from which many simple-to-follow but interesting and delicious recipes come—adapted this from Beth Hensberger's *The Bread Bible*.

"Bread" and "Bible": I like it. I've tweaked the instructions a bit. Thanks to both gals.

INGREDIENTS

2 packages (1½ tablespoons) active dry yeast
Pinch of sugar
½ cup warm water (105 to 115 degrees)
2 cups water
¼ cup molasses
¼ cup apple cider vinegar
4 tablespoons unsalted butter
1 ounce unsweetened chocolate
½ cup whole wheat flour
3 cups medium rye flour
3 cups unbleached, all-purpose or bread flour
1 cup bran

2 tablespoons caraway seeds
½ teaspoon fennel seeds
1 tablespoon salt
1 tablespoon instant espresso powder
1 tablespoon minced shallots
¼ cup cornmeal (optional)
1 tablespoon unbleached all-purpose flour (optional)
1 teaspoon caraway seeds (optional)

TO PREPARE

1. In a small bowl, combine yeast and sugar with warm water. Stir to dissolve and let stand until foamy, about 10 minutes.
2. Heat 2 cups water, molasses, vinegar, butter, and chocolate until the butter and chocolate are melted. Set aside.
3. Combine whole wheat, rye, and white flours in a large bowl. Set aside.
4. Combine 2 cups mixed flours, bran, caraway seeds, fennel seeds, salt, espresso, and shallots. Add yeast and chocolate mixtures. Knead until satiny and smooth, which will take several minutes. (You can also use one of those heavy mixers with a paddle attachment, but why? You can also grind the glorious whole gritty seeds in a spice grinder, coffee grinder, or mortar and pestle, but again, why?]
5. Add the remaining mixed flours half a cup at a time, until the dough clears the sides of the bowl. It will be very sticky but firm.
6. Flour the counter well, dump the dough onto it, and knead to make a springy yet dense dough.
7. Form the dough into a ball and place it in a greased bowl, turning so the whole ball is thoroughly greased. Cover with plastic wrap and let rise in a warm area (e.g. on top of a stove in which the oven is heated to 250 or so, or to the side of a fireplace in which a fire is lit, or near a space heater) until doubled, about 1½ to 2 hours. Combine cornmeal, flour, and remaining caraway seeds, if using, and set aside.
8. Gently punch down dough (self-explanatory: "punching down" is actually a term of art in bread-making). Turn the dough out onto a lightly floured surface. Divide into two portions and form into two rounds or loaves. Loaves should be placed in a loaf pan sprayed with nonstick spray, while rounds should be placed seam down on a greased or parchment-lined baking sheet. Sprinkle loaves with cornmeal

mixture, if using. Cover loosely with plastic wrap. Let rise until doubled in size, about 45 minutes to 1 hour. Slash a cross into the top of the round before baking.

9. Bake at 350 degrees for 45 to 50 minutes or until loaves are well-browned with a shiny crust. Remove from baking sheet to cool completely on a rack.

⇒ 2 ⇐

Existential Nostalgia

During the '50s and '60s, the metropolis of North Hampton, New Hampshire—my hometown—boasted a population of circa two thousand. Always on the kitchen counter at 108 Post Road was my mother's loose-leaf, red-and-white checked Betty Crocker cookbook: its pages pocked with shortening stains, vanilla extract droplets, and bits of cookie batter. Always the fridge held a bowl of cooked potatoes, left over from supper, to be made into home fries or patties. Always in the cupboard above the stove was a Crisco can of bacon grease, set on a pale green melamine plate to catch the drips, for frying potatoes or fish.

Mom was the original recycler.

My father cooked, too: corn fritters, clam chowder, bread. This was before the tiresome days when everything was a political "issue." Dad wasn't wildly concerned with "equality." He was a man and a lover of poetry and a construction worker and he just happened to like to cook.

Everything in our house was made from scratch. For breakfast, either Mom or Dad would make popovers, pancakes, muffins. Supper was meat loaf, lasagna, clams, haddock, flounder, lobster (my father had a little outboard motor and traps in the Hampton River). For dessert my mother made gingerbread with lemon sauce, peanut butter cookies with crisscrossed fork marks, apple pies with the outline of an apple knifed into the center of the crust. For snacks we had popcorn, popped in Mazola, or saltines crushed in a bowl of milk.

We shopped at the A&P; at the stand of Mr. Holman, the One-Armed Farmer; at Kennedy's Butter & Egg Store in Exeter for cottage cheese and freshly ground Eight O'Clock coffee. The country store at the bottom of the hill, a handy bike ride away, supplied penny candy, Black Jack gum, and Squamscot tonic (New Hampshirites call soda "tonic"). In summer, we'd sometimes pile in the car after supper and drive down Lafayette Road to the Big Scoop for ice cream in quintessentially New England flavors: frozen pudding, black raspberry, peppermint stick.

In retrospect this all sounds pretty idyllic, but as a child I was embarrassed by our failure to enter the Space Age. Why couldn't we have Tang and Rice-A-Roni and Cocoa Puffs like the other kids? Because that stuff was crap and my parents knew it (plus cooking from scratch was cheaper). Thanks to them, even today, I would rather not have brownies or pancakes or muffins at all than have them from a mix, rather use a teakettle than an electric kettle, rather heat something on the stove than in a microwave, rather peel and chop carrots, beets, fennel than buy a vacuum-packed cellophane package, rather forage fruit from a tree than buy it.

My scavenging skills were honed early. Walking the Atlantic shore, I grabbed handfuls of the amber-colored, gelatin-filled seaweed pods that draped the rocks and ate them. Exploring the wilderness behind our house, I gathered complimentary raspberries, fiddlehead ferns, and wild asparagus. Even now, I find free food a big draw—you never know when you're going to run out or get stranded or find yourself in jail—and always feel a little thrill at wrapping up a stray cookie or pizza crust and putting it in my pocket "for later."

Even now as well, I have a guilt-based fear of taking more than my share and a feeling close to compassion for food others might disdain. I'd almost rather eat slightly spoiled food, or leftovers, than high-end, over-priced food. I once drove cross-country and back subsisting for seven weeks on ak-mak crackers, sardines, and nuts. A samosa, cooked in a communal, grease-encrusted vat and sold by a crippled woman on the teeming streets of Calcutta, or a chunk of fresh sugarcane, chopped with a rusted machete by a sweating, shirtless chap on a polluted Thai beach I would fall upon with delight, but to patronize a Taco Bell or a Subway is a moral-aesthetic compromise I just can't, for the most part, bring myself to make.

I'm lucky enough to live in Southern California, home to some of the best farmers' markets, street food, and cutting-edge culinary trends in the

country. I can cook: roasted beet and blood orange salad, ricotta gnocchi with chanterelles and sweet corn, pine nut-polenta tart. But living alone, most of the time I graze: goat milk yogurt, dried apricots, almonds, arugula, St. André cheese, olives, an occasional slice of salami. I don't "locally source" all or even most of my food (much of which comes from Trader Joe's and an Armenian market in East Hollywood called Edi and Peter's). I rarely eat processed food—if for no other reason than that it doesn't taste good—but I take in my share of pesticides and chemicals along with the rest of the world. I splurge on an occasional high-end restaurant meal and I also pilgrimage a couple of times a week to the 99 Cents Only store on Sunset and Micheltorena.

I walk the mile each way because walking is a way to observe the world and give thanks. En route, I pay homage to the scarlet hibiscus, note the sun filtering through the amethyst bougainvillea, and smile at my fellow walkers. Inside the 99, I observe my fellow shoppers—old people, crazy people, punks, hipsters—and imagine their stories. I ponder the nobility of spirit of the minimum-wage cashiers who are efficient, forbearing, and kind. I give money to the homeless guys hanging out front.

Food, in other words, is about giving thanks, about the way we see and experience the world, about sharing.

I love food. What I abhor is food as fetish: chefs who objectify food in order to glorify themselves; food that is made to prostitute itself into something food was never meant to be: quail egg foam, liquid ham, garlic sorbet. I don't want ever to eat food that would be an insult to a starving person; that would be unrecognizable to a person who was truly hungry.

I also abhor supposed concern for the world that is really concern for ourselves: our health, our beauty, our longevity. As G. K. Chesterton observed: "There is more simplicity in the man who eats caviar on impulse than in the man who eats grape-nuts on principle." Or as Christ said, "Woe to you, scribes and Pharisees, you hypocrites. You cleanse the outside of cup and dish, but inside they are full of plunder and self-indulgence. Blind Pharisee, cleanse first the inside of the cup, so that the outside also may be clean" [Matthew 23:25–26].

Which is why I, for one, don't need precious, fussy "food rules": another province of the rich, and a variant form of fetishization. People have instinctively known what to eat, what they like, and what's good for them for thousands of years.

I don't need food rules: I need to get outdoors, observe the sky and trees and birds, and fully live. I need to be restored to the sanity of my deepest soul and heart. That so much of our food is engineered—and that so much of our food has become the province of pretentious, money-grubbing snobs—is emblematic of our cultural tendency to take the most sublime things on earth—food, sex, art—and try to sanitize, regulate, commodify, apply peer pressure to, and make money off them.

There's only one "rule" around food and that's whether whatever we happen to be tucking into at the moment evokes a spontaneous, *Man, is that good!*

◊ ◊ ◊ ◊

My childhood, like all childhoods, had its share of loneliness and sorrow. When I think back, though, one thing stands out: we ate supper together every night. I sincerely think that one consistent, communal event—which on many levels must have cost my overworked parents plenty—saved us, or at least saved me.

My father would have left for his bricklaying job in the dark and come home in the dark—and there he sat, with us. My mother would have washed, scrubbed, hung out clothes, folded, changed diapers, put kids down to nap, run errands, and cooked from the moment she awoke—and there she sat, with us. Way back then, I understood that my parents were laying down their lives so we could eat, and wear clothes, and have a roof over our heads. Way back then, I knew that the company is always higher than the food. Way back then, I learned that the spirit of the law is always higher than the letter.

As little Joe stabbed little Ross with a fork over the last hot dog, or two of us simultaneously lunged for the shepherd's pie, or a melee broke out over the discount brand harlequin ice cream, I knew to the marrow of my bones what I have never, in spite of every detour and wrong turn, for one minute doubted since: Love trumps all.

BETTY CROCKER'S BROWNIE PUDDING

God was in his heaven and all was right with the world the nights Mom made brownie pudding for dessert. This was one of the first recipes I learned to make on my own, using the battle-scarred 8 x 8-inch aluminum baking pan that also did duty for corn pudding for Thanksgiving, Yorkshire pudding to go with Dad's roast beef, and leftover squash, meat loaf or lasagna.

Brownie pudding, in case you don't know, has an upper layer of slightly crispy, cooked-batter brownie and a bottom layer of gooey liquid chocolate. Somehow this is achieved by the utterly unorthodox move of pouring a cup and a half of boiling water, mixed with brown sugar and cocoa powder, over the batter.

I've always wondered whether brownie pudding was the result of a happy mistake, like the discovery of penicillin. However it came into being, I can never hear the phrase, or imagine the meltingly rich taste, without feeling a warm rush of gratitude for my late, sainted mother.

INGREDIENTS

1 cup flour
3/4 cup sugar
2 tablespoons unsweetened cocoa powder
2 teaspoons baking powder
1/4 teaspoon salt
1/2 cup milk
2 tablespoons cooking oil
1 tablespoon vanilla
3/4 cup packed brown sugar
1/4 cup cocoa powder
1 1/2 cups boiling water

TO PREPARE

1. Grease or butter an 8 x 8-inch baking pan; either glass or metal is fine.
2. In a bowl, stir together the flour, sugar, baking powder, cocoa powder, and salt. Stir in milk, oil, and vanilla.
3. Pour batter into prepared baking pan. In a small bowl, stir together brown sugar and remaining 1/4 cup of cocoa powder. Stir in the boiling water. Slowly pour water mixture over batter.
4. Bake at 350 degrees for 40 minutes. Cool on a wire rack for 45–60 minutes. Serve warm with ice cream or whipped cream.

3

My Old Man

My father saw the world as a place of mystery and beauty, but that things could go so consistently, abysmally, wrong gnawed at him. His fertile imagination tended toward the catastrophic, and his saving grace was a black, self-deprecating sense of humor.

We had dinner—supper we called it—together every night. Around the table we bonded, made fun of each other, and endlessly squabbled. Around the table, neuroses were created and cemented in place with which I, for one, have struggled all my life. My older brother, Allen, and older sister, Jeanne, left home as soon as they graduated from high school, leaving me, at the age of ten, the oldest of the remaining six kids. My job, I believed, was to relieve my father's financial anxiety, and I took my position seriously. When he was worried, I was worried. Like my father, I took every wasted penny personally. Like my father, I learned early to see imaginary fissures in the seemingly solid facade of the world.

One night, the whole brood was eating supper and, as happened frequently, we ran out of milk. "I'll get some more," Ross (age eight at the time) offered, and made for the kitchen. Right away, Dad started in: "Don't drop the milk. For Crimey's sake, don't drop the milk, it's up to a dollar-thirty. Watch out Ross, whatever you do, don't drop the milk."

Almost inevitably, just as Ross was about to reach the table, he dropped the milk. A gallon of milk, released from the confines of its bottle, is a fearsome sight. With a tremendous crash, glass shattered, milk splashed,

milk pooled on the floor, milk ran in runnels into the kitchen. My father wasn't violent, but for a second noone breathed. Every pair of eyes, including Mom's, looked instinctively to the head of the table. A stricken, defeated look crossed Dad's face. Then he bent over double and silently buried his head in his hands.

Had we finally driven him over the brink? Had Dad lost it for good? What if he simply got up, donned his brown Carhartt jacket that smelled of White Owl cigars and Old Spice cologne, got in his pickup, and left? Who would take us out in the boat to check the banged-up lobster traps? Who would bake bread on weekends? Who would plant a single amaryllis bulb in a pot of soil, put it in the dining room window, and marvel when it bloomed each spring? Who would dig the garden, harvest the tomatoes, and sit out on the breezeway with his buddies drinking Bud listening to the Sox? Who would go around the house singing "When Irish Eyes are Smiling" in that crackpot fake tenor? Who would recite "And I am two-and-twenty,/And oh, 'tis true, 'tis true" from *A Shropshire Lad* with what sounded suspiciously like a catch in his throat? Mom *couldn't* leave us. But what if Daddy, fount of all fun, all jokes, all food, all security, bolted?

He was trembling, for God's sake! Was Dad *crying*? Had we made Daddy *cry*?

At last he straightened up. His beat-up hands dropped to his knees. His face, unthinkably, was wet with tears, and so red we thought he might have had a heart attack. He was still trembling. He was gasping. But finally we realized he wasn't crying. He was laughing.

"Ha ha, heh heh, Don't ... don't drop ... HAH ... HUNHH .... Janet, get me a napkin." He pointed to Ross, as if Ross had just told the funniest joke ever: "Don't spill ... HANH HAH ... if that doesn't beat .... HANNHHH .... Lindy Gilman's kids (Mr. Gilman was the Runnymede Farm milkman) will eat!" but he was laughing so hard he couldn't go on.

Suddenly we sprang into action. One of us ran to the rag box and started wiping up the spill. Someone else started picking out the biggest chunks of glass. Someone, maybe me, passed behind Dad's chair and patted his thinning hair.

But in a way, I am still sitting at that table with my father: head buried in his hands, present physically, yet a million miles away. Sitting with him while he contemplated the years behind and the years stretching ahead: of waking in the dark, of driving forty, sixty, ninety miles to work, of standing

CONTENTS

The discovery of a new dish does more for human happiness than the discovery of a new star.

ANTHELME BRILLAT-SAVARIN
Physiologie du Gout, 1825

For Joe-Joe, Roscoe, Geo, Wimble, and Little Meddy:
my first — and forever favorite — eating companions

famished

A FOOD MEMOIR WITH RECIPES

by HEATHER KING

in the bitter cold and scorching heat all day laying brick, of constant anxiety, constant frustration, constant fatigue.

Sitting with him knowing that when and if he opened his eyes his family, his glory and his cross, was going to be looking back at him: dependent, bereft, refusing to leave. Sitting with him while the people he loved most, and who were most bent, it must have seemed, on breaking his heart, held him to silent account. Sitting with him while all that was good and kind and decent in him, and all that was fearful and weak and in pain had perhaps met, and clashed. Sitting with him while, in some place that was unknown to us, where we could not follow, on some terrible battlefield in which our fates hung in the balance, he had chosen us over himself; had chosen the spark of life that is humor over despair; over death.

In a way, that is who I write for. My father—and all fathers like him— in that moment before he lifted his head, and stayed.

For weeks we'd be finding splinters of glass under the sewing table, the desk, the radiators. There would be more anxiety. There would be more pain. But for now, we were saved. For now—until the next broken bottle of milk, or window, or leg, or spirit—life could go on.

Because Dad had laughed. Thank God Almighty. Daddy had laughed.

FALL SLAW WITH APPLES AND BACON

When we were kids on the New Hampshire coast, my father made coleslaw from green cabbage and carrots, grated in a metal food grinder he clamped to the counter edge like a vise, then mixed with store-bought mayonnaise, celery seed, and a splash of lemon juice. It was darn tasty, and went well with the flounder, haddock, and clams we often caught ourselves and ate for supper.

This is a slightly fancier version that stays true to its roots by availing itself of whatever would be likely to be loitering in the average fridge at any given time: a stray half-cabbage, the last quarter pound of bacon, a couple of borderline-crystallized tablespoons at the bottom of a jar of honey. It's sturdy enough to stand as a meal in itself, and it also goes well with eggs, a burger, or fish.

We wouldn't have had shallots in my childhood kitchen, but certainly we would have had all the other ingredients: cabbage, cider vinegar, apples, celery, and always, thanks be to heaven, bacon.

INGREDIENTS

6 tablespoons cider vinegar

1 tablespoon plus 1 teaspoon red wine vinegar

3 tablespoons water

3 tablespoons oil

3 tablespoons minced shallots

2 tablespoons plus 2 teaspoons honey

½ teaspoon coarse salt

Red pepper flakes, to taste

12 cups ⅓ inch sliced mixed cabbage, such as red, green, and savoy

2 tart apples, quartered, cored, grated, shredded, or minced

¾ cup small-diced celery

¼ cup snipped chives

7 bacon slices, cooked until crisp but not burnt, crumbled

(I've never followed any of these amounts to the letter. As long as you don't overdo the red wine vinegar, you'll be fine.)

TO PREPARE

1. Make the dressing: measure the cider, red wine vinegar, water, oil, shallots, honey, salt, and red pepper flakes into a small bowl and whisk until combined.
2. Place the cabbage, apples, celery, and chives in a large bowl. Add the dressing. Toss until coated. (This can be made a day ahead and refrigerated to let the flavors mellow.)
3. Serve chilled or room temperature, as you prefer (I happen to like room temperature). Just before serving, add the crumbled bacon and toss well. You'll want to taste now to adjust the oil, honey, and/or vinegar as necessary. Serve immediately—you want the bacon to still be crisp.)

❧ 4 ❧

Apprentice

I taught myself to cook in my early twenties from two books: *The Tassajara Bread Book* by Edward Espe Brown, and *The Vegetarian Epicure*, by Anna Thomas. They were California cookbooks and they went well with the artists I worshiped at the time: Joni Mitchell, Lawrence Ferlinghetti, Jack Kerouac. I saw that watching a recipe come together was catch-your-breath exciting, like watching a photo develop. I saw that anyone with a knife, a spoon, a modicum of patience, and a love for food can cook.

I had a surfer boyfriend—thus, someone to cook *for* at the time—and that helped. When you're in love with a person, you tend to be in love with everything: learning, chopping vegetables, washing dishes, and especially eating. I remember standing in the open kitchen of the apartment we shared, watching Watergate on TV and making Roquefort mousse, sauce aurore, potage les deux champignons, and peach kuchen.

The whole time I was learning to cook (in fact, for the duration of my fifteen-year drinking career), I waitressed.

I was a terrible waitress: surly, hungover, ADD. I hadn't yet learned that real love, authentic love, extends to everyone, not just, say, the person you happen to be sleeping with. I actually did want to do a good job, but I probably owe amends to about 80 percent of the people I ever "served." I still have anxiety dreams about the restaurants where I worked: Lomazzo's (Hampton Beach), the Seagull Diner (Kittery, Maine), and Legal Sea Foods, Jimbo's Fish Shanty, Charlie's Beef 'n' Beer, and Sam's Beef and

Ale (Boston; that last *after* I got my law degree).

My fellow workers formed a kind of surrogate (and highly dysfunctional) family. As in team sports, the shared goal built camaraderie. As in war, the stress and uncertainty, the opportunity for grace under fire, the dehumanization of the enemy—the enemy to my mind being the bosses, and often, the customers—forged a powerful bond. Add to that the prospect of nightly tips/booze money, and for an addict, you've got yourself a job that's irresistibly love-hate compelling.

I used to think I chose waitressing because I made fresh drinking money every night, or to be around booze, but probably the real draw was the free food: food filched from customers' plates on the way from kitchen to table, food fished from bus buckets, food swiped from backroom refrigerators. Thirty-plus years later, I called a former boss to offer to reimburse him for all the cocktail shrimp I stole from the walk-in and ate on the job. He never picked up and I don't blame him.

I had no feel for service work, but I have great, great respect for the waitresses, busboys, diner cooks, and convenience store clerks who do. I have a friend who, when the economy tanked, had to sell his bookstore and train for a job at 7-Eleven. He told me, "You can't believe the amount of stuff you have to keep straight: lottery tickets, phone cards, Slurpees, Big Gulps." He has an IQ of probably 140 and he was fired after a week.

Restaurant work, like all service work, is a vocation. I'm glad, for everyone's sake, I moved on to an apprenticeship at my real vocation. But—though I found another way to make amends—I still feel a little bit bad about those shrimp.

SMOKED BLUEFISH PÂTÉ

Adapted from *The New Legal Sea Foods Cookbook*
by Roger Berkowitz & Jane Doerfer

(Legal, which is now a nationwide empire, sells the pâté ready-made. You can buy it online as of this writing for $16.99 a pound plus $25 shipping. But what fun would that be?)

Back in the day, blues, which we used to catch with drop lines off the side of my father's boat in the Hampton River, were almost a trash fish. Like mackerel, bluefish is oily, which takes well to smoking.

To check on the availability and price, I consulted with my commercial fisherman brother, Geordie, who's run a boat out of Portsmouth, New Hampshire for over thirty years. He replied:

"Bluefish is still fairly abundant from the Carolinas up to New England, mostly during the warmer summer months. We catch quite a few on the party boats in say late July and August. Some years there're plenty of them and other years they are a complete no-show here. Mostly dependent upon weather and water temps. I'd say during the summer they're typically $3.50–$5.00 a pound of fillets at the fish market, but you won't find them in fish markets around here until summer, so they're really a seasonal species. Yes, we did use to catch them from Dad's boat at times, but we did more mackerel and flounder fishing. Hope this answers your question. Until we speak again, fair winds and following seas, lassy!"

Smoked bluefish now costs as much as $39.99 a pound, depending on whether you can find it in your local fish store or have to buy it online. If you live in New England, your local fish store may carry it. Or you could buy it in a local market for, say, eight bucks a pound and smoke it yourself (you know how to do that, right?)

Otherwise, Chowhound is a great online resource for tracking down hard-to-find items and learning where they may be sold locally.

And sometimes recipes are simply to read, enjoy, reminisce over, or dream on.

INGREDIENTS

1 pound smoked bluefish fillet
½ pound cream cheese
¼ cup butter (half a stick), room temperature
3 tablespoons minced shallots
2 tablespoons Cognac
2 tablespoons freshly squeezed lemon juice
1 teaspoon Worcestershire sauce
Freshly ground pepper
Chopped toasted walnuts or hazelnuts

TO PREPARE

1. Purée bluefish, cream cheese, butter and Cognac in food processor. Add shallots, lemon juice and Worcestershire. Pulse processor on and off to combine. You want the pâté smooth but with a bit of texture. Season with sea salt and freshly ground pepper. Pack into a crock or soufflé dish, or mound over salad greens and garnish with herbs, raw vegetables, or seaweed. (Come on, folks, be creative!) Serve with water crackers or melba toast.

Makes about 4 cups. The pâté will keep in the fridge for four or five days.

≫ 5 ≪

Dream House

For six years in the late '70s and early '80s I lived in Boston's old West End at 121 Merrimac Street, a shabby wedge-shaped brick building that had originally been a textile factory and was at that point one of the city's last remaining single-room occupancies. The back alley dumpsters swarmed with rats, men in motorcycle jackets and leather caps blasted disco music in the S & M gay bar downstairs till two in the morning, and in the five floors above, alcoholics, drug addicts and the mentally ill rented rooms by the night or week.

I felt at home in my loft for, from my earliest memories, I, too, had felt deficient in some fundamental, shameful way; unequipped to function in an alien world. I had drunk my way through high school, drunk my way through college, and drunk my way through law school. At last I reached a point where I was no longer educable and no longer employable. I no longer bothered even to pretend that I was capable of quitting. Drinking was my purpose, my religion, what I was compelled to do, day in, day out, without question or surcease.

I lived during those years in a state of excruciating, desperate longing. I did not know it for a long time later, but it was the longing of the leper, the paralytic, the demoniac, the ones who thirsted and crawled and dragged themselves along with makeshift staffs and withered legs; the hemorrhaging woman who touched the hem of Christ's robe and was healed.

Those were thin years for cooking. I had a hot plate and a toaster oven.

I ate at the restaurants where I waitressed. I ate beer nuts. I ate maraschino cherries scarfed from bartenders' caddies. I ate onion rings from Buzzy's Roast Beef in three a.m. blackouts.

I brought home strangers, the experience lost in a blackout haze, leaving me shaking and hungover the next morning, crazed with loneliness, wondering if there was a mathematical concept known as negative zero, an emptiness never filled, but multiplied to infinity.

In the back of the freezer, I found a chicken pot pie I'd bought months ago, stabbed it with a fork and tossed it into the toaster oven, its dented tray blanketed with burnt crumbs. Starving, I took it out early, picked off the edges of the crust and, unable to wait, wolfed down the rest, the middle still raw, the peas partly frozen, my first solid food in days, feeling my strength coming back, using the crinkly aluminum dish for an ashtray, stubbing out Winstons in the streaky yellow gravy, pouring a slug of gin into a Flintstones glass, putting on *Aretha's Greatest Hits*.

After a while, it started to get light. I could make out the outline of the Lindemann Mental Health Center across the street, the sky a bruise and, if I opened the window at the end of the hall, a gust of cold air blew in carrying the metallic smell of rain.

◊ ◊ ◊ ◊

I started drinking in the morning. When I came to at four, or five, or six, I started begging my neighbor Sonny, also a total alkie, to sell me a couple of cans of Black Label: a buck apiece he charged me. I started frequenting the old men's bars around North Station—Sullivan's Tap, the Iron Horse—that opened at eight a.m. Every object seemed freighted with a burning lucidity, as if the world were about to burst into flame: the terror of existing, the incomprehensibility of suffering, the hopelessness of escape. The crushed-out cigarettes beside my bed marked the wasted hours, the spent ash my life consuming itself in swirls of acrid blue smoke.

One month I missed my period. I bought the home test at Stop & Shop, woke up the next morning, stared in shock and dread to find the water bright blue.

The clinic was cold. My legs were goosebumped, my feet were purple, the paper johnny rustled and scratched. I watched the holes in the ceiling tiles while they worked between my legs with their cold jellies and their cold, businesslike hands, and when the pain started, I closed my eyes. They called it a procedure, but a procedure was a dental implant or a hip replacement, a move forward, a celebration of continued life, where afterwards you might be given an extracted tooth, a piece of abraded bone, as a memento of your bravery. They didn't do that there, though. They gave me a couple of Chips Ahoy and a Kotex and a cot to lie on for a few minutes, and then I got up to make room for the next girl and took the Green Line back to Merrimac Street, alone.

◊ ◊ ◊ ◊

I was thirty-three when I took my last drink. The questions I had avoided for so long—where I had come from, where I was going, my purpose on earth—began to present themselves as of vital importance. I knelt on the splintery boards beside my bed and began, awkwardly, to pray.

Over the course of the next two years, I got a job as a real estate title examiner, started paying off my student loan, made friends with other sober alcoholics. Inchoate ideas swirled up from my subconscious: that there had been a reason for my suffering, that some cosmic, flesh-and-blood presence had been suffering along with me.

A man I'd known since high school asked me to marry him, and one afternoon he and several old, mutual friends from New Hampshire drove down to Merrimac Street in a white ice cream truck to move me out. I'd packed hurriedly: papers from law school and coat hangers stuffed helter-skelter into one box; sweaters, frying pans and my hair dryer in another. After awhile we got sick of lugging things five flights down and walking five flights back up, so someone rigged up a makeshift pulley and started lowering the big items down by rope: my old scarred bureau, minus drawers, like an old man with his teeth out; the desk I'd inherited from my grandmother descending upside down, its legs waving in the air; the refrigerator, naked and defenseless, like a slug coaxed from its shell.

When the last sagging box and plastic garbage bag had been hauled down, I went back up one more time, alone. There was a blank space on the floor where my mattress had lain, rectangles of dust under the dresser that hadn't been moved in six years, heaps of cockroach husks in the corners I thought I'd cleaned.

I closed both windows, Sonny came over in his underwear to hug me goodbye and, finally, it was time to go.

Out on the sidewalk, someone said, "Can you believe you're getting out of this dump for good?"

"Yeah," I laughed wanly, "what a dump," but the whole time as we got into the truck, drove down Causeway past Dunkin' Donuts and the pawn shop and Sullivan's Tap, crossed north over the Mystic River Bridge, I felt shaky and stubborn inside, like a child who's trying not to cry.

These were kind, decent people I had known since I was twelve, who had been blessed with confidence, savvy, social grace, who wanted the best for me, too. How could I explain that failure and ineptitude were their own kinds of gifts? How could I tell them that in the heart of that shabby room I had found God?

I thought I had left Merrimac Street behind forever that day, but all these years later, it still haunts my dreams: the sink with its necklace of cigarette burns, the drifts of cat hair in the hallway, Sonny holding a can of beer aloft like a chalice. When I wake, in that split second before I am torn from sleep, I think, *I am loved. I have always been loved.*

BANANA BUTTERMILK PANCAKES

You don't want a super-complicated "breakfast" recipe when you're insanely hungover. Whatever time of the day or night you come to, you want a cheap, consoling, comforting meal that can be cooked on a hotplate. Pancakes, for instance.

Made-from-scratch pancakes were a frequent breakfast item in our house. One of us would have put out plates, silverware, paper napkins, and butter. We had an electric griddle, its surface blackened with use, that Mom or Dad would bring in, plug into the socket beneath the picture window, and cook on right from the table. We might have corn pancakes, blueberry pancakes, apple pancakes or banana pancakes.

You can add any kind of fruit (or even vegetable) you like to a basic pancake recipe. I've used bananas below but you can leave them out or substitute. Tiny pockets of raw batter will form around the pieces of whatever you're using, so make sure you cut them up fairly small.

The chances that a drunk would have a banana (or flour, or an egg) on hand, are slim to none, but if you happen to, these are simple to whip up. And if even making a batch of pancakes is too much, you can always just drink some maple syrup straight from the bottle, for a sugar kick, before heading down to the bar.

And don't forget, if you're sick and tired of being sick and tired, there is help! Go to the very front of the phone book, first letter, first entry almost, and give those folks a shout.

INGREDIENTS

1 cup all-purpose flour
1 teaspoon baking soda
½ teaspoon salt
1 egg, lightly beaten
1 cup milk, buttermilk, or yogurt
1 mashed-up overripe banana, or sliced regular banana
Vegetable, olive, or motor oil (whoops!) for griddle

TO PREPARE

1. Throw all the ingredients together into a bowl and stir with a spoon, whisk, or pair of chopsticks till mixed.
2. Put your frying pan on the hotplate, turn on to medium high, let the pan get fairly hot, and pour on a tablespoon or so of oil. Then pour a quarter of a cup of batter, plus or minus, on the griddle in rounds or squiggles or pentagrams. Turn when the underside is crispy brown, if possible meanwhile minimizing spills of cigarette ash and cheap bourbon on your breakfast-to-be. Caution: do not pass out while Side Two is cooking, or at any other time while the hotplate is on.
3. I don't need to tell you to slather with butter and real maple syrup. If you're buying that gruesome Aunt Jemima dreck, go straight to rehab.

≫ 6 ≪

A Good Appetite

An interview with author and podcaster
Tara Rodden Robinson

TARA*: One spiritual imperative is feeding the hungry. What are people starving for? How do we, as followers of Christ, offer different kinds of "food" to address those kinds of starvation?*

I love food. Shopping for it, talking about it, cooking it, sharing it, eating it, reading about it. Food to me is a sacrament. A sacrament is something that signifies that which it brings into being. An embraces signifies love and it brings into being more love. Food signifies nourishment and love and, treated properly, it brings into being more love. Culturally, we have made food into an anti-sacrament. The poor are starving and the rich are making food into nonfood foams and gels, holding contests to see how fast they can cook, elevating chefs and their personalities to cult status—that to me is a sacrilege. That doesn't interest me at all. It's food porn. It's de-sacramentalizing food.

Einstein said, "Strive not to be a success, but rather to be of value." You can be technically the best chef in the world but if you don't know how to welcome a guest, you have missed the mark. Your food might be a success but it has no value.

One of my favorite food writers, A. J. Liebling, has a wonderful essay called "A Good Appetite." In it his friend, a fellow Parisian gourmand is dying—not, by Liebling's lights, from too much rich food, but from the man's hovering wife who, concerned about his health, is depriving him of all his favorite dishes. Liebling continues quaffing champagne and putting away six-course luncheons; the abstemious friend, sequestered in his lavish apartment, wastes away. There's a line that, to me, pulls the whole essay together. Liebling writes: "Once, being in his quarter in the company of a remarkably pretty woman, I called [my friend] up, simply because I knew he would like to look at her, but he was too tired."

Now that's a friend! And that the beautiful woman was willing to be brought by to please an elderly dying gourmand is sheer class. When we deprive ourselves of beautiful food out of a picky concern for our health, we close ourselves off to all kinds of other legitimate pleasures. The old guy had become too weak to appreciate a good-looking woman! Have some oysters, for heaven's sake!

Also, you just know the food Liebling is writing about, and the chefs who cooked it ... there was a sacrifice involved. The right kind of pride yes, but also humility. You bow in a sense before the blue trout and the God who's given you the talent and heart to learn how to properly cook it; you don't force your guests to bow before you. That's what's missing from the way we approach food today. Cooking has become about money and fame. Not that "celebrity chefs" don't work hard, but the purpose of the work often seems to be to achieve personal status, not to glorify the food and the communion that food rightly brings.

The purpose of being a cook is to make people feel welcome, not to make them feel afraid they won't "get" the food, to make them self-conscious that they're not part of some rarefied circle of connoisseurs. I once went to some faux hoity-toity Italian restaurant in West Hollywood where the whole obsequious feel of the place was insufferable. I ordered linguini with white clam sauce and when I asked for parmesan the waiter acted, as I knew he would, like I'd suggested pouring ketchup on caviar. I said politely, "I know cheese with white clam is frowned upon but I like it." And the guy was a total jackass about it. Shaming. That's the kind of thing I'm talking about. Listen, this wasn't a 1904 bottle of Château d'Yquem. It was a plate of pasta, at a mid-range, run-of-the-mill, pretentious chophouse, a cut or two above Olive Garden. If I'm willing to look like a rube, that's my business. And for a waitperson to be a jackass is way more classless than not to "know" about food. What if the customer had been someone's grandmother who, at great expense and great sacrifice, had made a once-in-

Heather King ◊ 31

a-lifetime trip to Los Angeles? Give her the freakin' cheese, treat her like royalty, and say a little prayer she has a good time.

To look at beauty, food, and all of life as a generosity, a sharing, is deeply incarnational. Food—the shared meal, the Eucharist, the banquet table— is central to us incarnate beings. At the same time, "Man does not live by bread alone." Catholicism is extravagant and sensual but it is never merely extravagant, nor sensual for sensuality's sake. We can be profligate, and we can also be ascetic. We can feast and, when need be, we can fast: we can do without for the sake of the other.

So the question is always how can we feed each other spiritually, whether we're literally feeding each other a meal or whether we're writing, reading, walking, driving, talking, listening, or sitting by the bedside of a sick friend.

As Catholics, we participate in consuming the body of Christ in the Eucharist. How has that fed you? What has that fed in you?

To me, Christ is the Alpha and the Omega, the ground of all existence. So the Eucharist is everything. Christ says, "If you have seen me, you have seen the Father." This is a stupendous statement. It means God literally walked the earth, walks it still. *And He has given us Himself to eat.* It's a scandal. It's utterly weird and somehow utterly right. No human being would have come up with such an idea of God on his own. When we love someone, in a sense we want to consume them. Jeffrey Dahmer ate his victims because, as he said, "That way, they couldn't leave me." This is shades of the Eucharist; passion obviously gone way, way over to pathology. But that thin line between the two fascinates me.

You have to be kind of crazy to love Christ. The neighbors thought Christ was crazy. The saints are partly crazy. Who's going to even try to love their enemies? Who's going to even entertain the notion of taking last place instead of jockeying for first? Who's going to eat the Body and drink the Blood of God? To believe in the Real Body and the Real Blood is to know that Christ was not just a "great teacher." Christ was not just another "moral leader." Love thine enemies was not a figure of speech, a nice little theory for the dreamers of the world. He meant every single thing that he said. Do good to those who hate you. Bless those who persecute you. Love one another as I have loved you. These are not cozy little sentiments. They are the Way, the Truth, and the Life because following those teachings is the only way we are going to be able to get along together long enough to save the world. They are the only way we can hope to live in any kind of freedom and joy.

And they mean Crucifixion and Resurrection: dying to our way to be born into a new way. Make no mistake: narrow is the gate. As G. K. Chesterton observed, "It's not that Christianity has been tried and found wanting; it's that it's never been tried." Abandoning our will goes profoundly against our grain; against what seems to "make sense."

What *seems* to make sense is violence. What seems to makes sense is stockpiling, hoarding, and dominating.

What does it mean to "hunger and thirst for righteousness?"

Being crazy enough to let our desire—for connection, to love and to be loved—go to the stars. To let ourselves feel the pain of our holy longing for transcendence.

I was very very lucky to come to Christ through my alcoholism. For twenty years total I was a hard-core, falling-down, black out drunk. When I got sober, I saw that in spite of my egregious shortcomings, wrong turns, and extremely bad track record in the bars, I had been the recipient of unmerited mercy.

You can't be the recipient of that kind of grace without very soon seeing how you have contributed to the suffering of the world and wanting very much to begin trying to alleviate it. Part of what I sobered up to is the fact that we are all deeply, intricately connected. What I eat matters. What I say, think, do matters. Prayer matters. That's the doctrine of the Mystical Body of Christ. We're all part of one another. Everything we do affects everyone else. We're called to bear the huge gap between who we wish we were and who we actually are; between the world as we long for it to be and the world as it actually is. If you're at all tuned in to your own suffering, your own loneliness, you begin to be tuned in to the suffering of the world. That is the deepest reality, the deepest truth: the bleeding wound at the heart of mankind that no amount of social justice or legislation can cure. It's a wound of exile, of abandonment. Christ on the Cross is in solidarity with that wound.

I'm not worse than anyone else, but I'm not any better either. I'm called to see the people who do evil in the world as my brothers and sisters. I'm not above them. I've done evil myself. That's not to overfocus on the negative;

it's to acknowledge the human condition and to be in right relationship with reality, which is continual hunger, famine, and war, both literal and figurative. Our hearts are all hungry and we are all at war with ourselves and our neighbor. We are all, in the deepest human sense, alone. *And we all know we're going to die.*

When you tap into that mother wound of sorrow ... if not for the Eucharist, I feel like we would simply have to die of sorrow; of our inability to heal all the suffering of the world, of the babies starving to death, the children being beaten, of the endless, endless misery, sickness, violence, and poverty. The Eucharist says, the poor you will always have with you—but Christ also says in so many words, do one little thing today and that will go towards healing everything. Keep your big sarcastic mouth shut when the sharp retort is on the tip of your tongue. Let someone else go first in line. Bless the hipster who throws you an imperious look, bless the guy who almost runs you down in the crosswalk. I, for one, will have to process my hurt and anger first. I'll have to acknowledge, one more time, all the times I've cast imperious looks and almost run people down in crosswalks.

We get to enjoy our food, give thanks for it, and notice what we eat because it's beautiful and it's good, even if it's a handful of crackers and a few dried figs, and we are beyond blessed to have it. We get to share our food, our money, our time, our joy, our energy. Give a few bucks to the homeless woman. Work in the soup kitchen if that's our thing. In my case, the thing is to write and speak and answer endless emails and prayer requests. My life is nothing in the eyes of the world and everything in God's eyes.

I'm trying to experience my physical body as a temple. Given that food is essential for life, how can we make eating an act of worship and love for God?

I think we make love, not health, the measure. Food is above all to be enjoyed. I don't own a pair of bathroom scales. I seldom read the fat labels. In one way, I'm extremely non-fussy about what I eat. My measure is: *Does it taste good?* Not: Is it gluten-free, is it organic, does it have more than two grams of transfat or whatever. My question is: *Do I love it?* Consequently I eat relatively well without spending a whole lot of time thinking and planning, because bad food doesn't taste good.

I'm not going to eat fast food or processed food because the whole idea of genetically modified, laboratory-engineered food in grotesquely huge portions is offensive to my spirituality, to my love of beauty and fairness and generosity and kindness and goodness. But mostly, the food doesn't taste good. Nor does eating more than what's good for me feel good. Left to our own devices, we have an internally sound, self-regulating voice.

It's the same with books. I was talking to someone recently who said her Bible group was carefully compiling a list of approved books and my response was, "You'll know what to read because books that are not about the glorious, sublimely tormented/conflicted human condition will be BORING." I don't want to read soft-core porn, I don't want to read gothic lite about vampires, I don't want to read self-promotional agitprop, I don't want New Age dreck, I don't want salacious gossip. I don't have the time, the patience, or the interest. Just as you naturally won't eat crap, you naturally won't read crap. But you have to be willing to live in enough silence and solitude that you can "hear" that inner voice. The more attuned you are to that moral-aesthetic compass, the less time and energy you'll have to spend agonizing about what you're going to eat or read.

My eating habits, like most everyone's, were very much formed in my childhood. There were eight of us kids and there was actually a bit too little food to go around. So even now, I tend to unconsciously eat a teeny bit less than what will fully sate me. I don't like to be stuffed. I like to be always a little bit hungry. Which has turned out to be a good thing, because that's how you totally enjoy your food. Everything tastes SO GOOD. Also, that way you're always ready for a feast.

Trust me, you invite me over for dinner, I am into it! I'm first in line. I'm there for seconds. I enjoy my food, and I'm thankful for it, and the ideal guest to me is the one who volunteers to go first because he can hardly contain his enthusiasm! I'd rather fast completely than do this horrible, picky, *Oh I'm dieting. I'm not eating sugar this week.* Well stay home then!— we're not here to order the evening to your self-involved dietary regimen.

Here's another scenario: Have you ever had a hostess prepare a big delicious meal and then when everyone sits down refuse herself to eat? Now that to me is hostile. I want to watch you eat but I myself am not going to eat. I want you to get fat but I'm going to stay skinny. Or whatever is going through her (and it is always a her that pulls that particular stunt) mind. I don't know what that is but to me it's kind of anti-food, anti-sacrament. At my house ... I mean, I'm polishing off my own meal and then I'm picking food off your plate! I'm eating with my fingers and talking a mile a minute and keeping an eye out for who needs what and making sure everyone is included in the conversation.

I'm no fan of control, as in birth control, gun control, food control. Either you're for all of life or you're not for life at all. Throw all the guns away; get married and have tons of sex and the kids that go along with it; eat what you want and take a walk every day, reveling in the light, the sun, the sky, the flowers. Catholicism is extravagant, profligate. There's nothing stuffy or uptight or creepy or weird about the love of Christ. We love food, we love sex! We love it so much we willingly put a frame around it and the frame is love. Love saves self-denial, asceticism, and taking up our cross from being masochistic or self-depriving. A new mother is going without sleep, regular meals, any semblance of her old routine, but we would never think of her as *ascetic*. Out of love we will do without all kinds of things that we wouldn't dream of calling sacrifice.

You can't pluck "health" out of the lineup of your life as if it were some separate hothouse flower. Health is a by-product of community. And true health is about more fun, more laughter, more people, more good food, not less. I would rather live in abundance and joy and live a shorter amount of time than live in some weird, cold, controlled, fear-based, peer pressure-based prison around food and everything else and live to be a hundred. Big deal if you've managed and controlled your whole life: you've never fully lived one second. Get out on the street! Eat a greasy taco from the roach coach. Pick an avocado that's fallen from the tree off the sidewalk and dig in.

True health also doesn't cost a lot of money. I have been felled by sickness, a flu of some sort, I think once in the last ten years (that's not counting my cancer, which I basically ignored and it went away). I drink coffee, I eat sugar. I love bread, pasta, cheese. I'm 5 feet 6 and I probably weigh 115. I go to the gym every other day or so and lift a few weights. I take a walk on the other days. Walking is the single most brilliant exercise. I hesitate to even call it that. It's what I love to do. It's a treat. Mentally, physically, emotionally, spiritually. I often take the same walk every day and I never get tired of it! I have certain flowers and shrubs and weeds and trees I love along the way. I think about my work. I get insights. I pray for people. I smile at strangers. I study the light. This is in the middle of Los Angeles! You don't need fancy equipment or clothes or even shoes to be in perfectly good health and shape.

We get to train our eyes to see the crazy beauty everywhere. Everything becomes an act of praise; everything becomes a way of seeking God, connecting with God, learning about God. Laughing at ourselves. We get to wear the world like a loose garment.

I love an occasional feast, but day by day I more or less live on dried fruit, nuts, cheese, flatbread, yogurt. A piece of fish, a roast chicken every few weeks. Olives, feta, greens. But I'm also not "above" eating a Big Mac with fries and one of those chemical apple pies once or twice a year AT ALL. I've driven cross-country a couple of times and I remember outside Charleston, West Virginia, once, I was starving. I pulled into a McDonald's right off the freeway, and I was just shaking with gratitude and relief as I tore into that cheeseburger. There was this middle-aged waitress, overweight with sores on her legs and a red polo shirt and one of those ridiculous baseball caps they make the workers wear, who had the kindest, most long-suffering face. I watched her as she took and prepared my order, and she was totally courteous and decent and patient and kind. That is nobility of spirit, man, and I've remembered her ever since because in the end, that *is* what you remember: goodness. Making minimum wage, supporting a meth-head kid or two … these are the people who are last here and in heaven will be first. Those are the people to whom I genuflect. Not some blowhard celebrity chef. The single mothers who have to work at MacDonald's and are still kind.

CHICKEN LEGS WITH KUMQUATS, PRUNES, AND GREEN OLIVES

Adapted from *The Santa Monica Farmers' Market Cookbook*,
by Amelia Saltsman

Doesn't that sound awful? *Au contraire*, I'm telling you, this recipe is utterly delicious, and I include it as an example of God's ever-creative bounty. The tenderly stewed chicken, the tang of citrus, the richness of dark prunes, the Mediterranean sun-kissed depth of green olives: the whole makes for a visual and gustatory delight that's easy to cook and a surprise all the way around. I first made this for a dinner party. The guests were bowled over.

Kumquats, ovoid, bright orange-gold citrus the size of kalamata olives, are in season January through March and sometimes into April. I usually get them in Asian markets here in LA, a pound or two in a rectangular cellophane box. They're not expensive. You can pop them in your mouth whole, skin and all, for a mini-explosion of sweet fruit contrasting with pucker-sour peel.

INGREDIENTS

½ *pound prunes*
½ *cup boiling water*
½ *pound kumquats*
1 *tablespoon olive oil*
2–4 *whole chicken legs*
Sea salt
Ground black pepper
1 *chopped large onion*
2 *cloves garlic*
¾ *cup dry white wine*
1 *cup mildish green olives*
½ *cup chicken stock*
Harissa (a Tunisian hot chile pepper paste, optional)

TO PREPARE

1. Pour the half cup of boiling water over the prunes to soften, and let sit 15 minutes. Drain and pit and quarter the prunes (tip: use scissors).

Quarter the dear little kumquats lengthwise, remove the seeds and white pith, and cut the quarters in half again lengthwise. Set the prunes and kumquats aside.

2. In a wide pot, heat the oil over medium heat. Working in batches if necessary to avoid crowding, add the chicken pieces, season with salt and pepper, and brown, turning as needed, until golden on all sides, 10–12 minutes. Remove the chicken to a plate. Pour off all but 1–2 tablespoons of the fat from the pot, reduce the heat to medium-low, and add the onion. Stir well, scraping any brown bits from the bottom of the pan, and cook, stirring occasionally, until the onion is translucent and soft, 5–7 minutes. Add the garlic, stir, and cook for another 1 minute. Add the wine, raise the heat to medium, and cook, stirring to deglaze the pot (deglaze means to loosen food particles from and add liquid to, so as to make a sauce), until the liquid is reduced by slightly more than half, about 3 minutes. Return the chicken to the pot and add the prunes, kumquats, olives, and salt and pepper to taste. Stir, cover, reduce the heat to low, and simmer for 20 minutes.

3. Add ¼ cup of the stock, stir (the sauce will develop and thicken as the chicken cooks), and simmer covered until the chicken is very tender, about an hour, basting occasionally with the sauce and adding stock as needed so that the chicken is half submerged in the sauce for the duration of cooking time.

4. Serve with couscous or rice, a green salad, and (optionally) harissa.

≫ 7 ≪

Everyone's So Fat

LA is the last place I ever thought I'd end up. Though I'd never felt particularly at home in New England, back in 1990 LA seemed more of an idea—a really bad idea—than an actual place. My older brother Allen, who'd been a building contractor in Manhattan Beach for twenty years, seemed to bear out my worst suspicions. Whenever he came back east to visit, he went around in his Cole Haan loafers and eighty-dollar haircut saying, "Everything's so small! Everyone's so fat!" *What a snob*, I used to think.

As it turned out, Allen was the main reason my husband Tim and I ended up moving to LA. At the time, we were living on Boston's North Shore, Tim was a carpenter, and I was trying to work up the courage to 1) start using the law degree I'd earned in an alcoholic blackout; 2) start writing; and 3) start over. When we got married in 1988, Allen gave us weeklong round-trip tickets to LA as a wedding present.

It was sweet of him to invite us to stay with him and his wife in Manhattan Beach, but we felt lost among all those perfectly toned women with ponytails hanging out of the back of their Gold's Gym baseball caps, all those jocks with white teeth and chiseled biceps who looked like extras from Hawaii Five-0. Everything about us seemed inadequate for LA, or at least that part of LA: we didn't care enough about what kind of car we drove, didn't like to shop enough, weren't perky and upbeat enough. Still, Allen kept urging us, "You should move out here. The weather's beautiful. There's tons of money. I'll even give Tim (who is now my ex-husband) a job."

Almost everything about Los Angeles seemed wrong, but we came anyway. Maybe it was the birds-of-paradise and Mexican sage and bougainvillea, maybe it was that we both knew there weren't that many more years in which we might have the energy and impetus to make a major move, maybe in the end it was the light: so seductive, so beckoning, so full of hope. When we first moved, to a rented house in the Culver City neighborhood of Palms, I got a load of the cars shining in the driveways, the shady green lawns, and the first night propped my bike against an angel-pink oleander in the side yard and went to bed. The bike was gone in the morning, of course, a perfect introduction to the *trompe l'oeil* contradictions with which every Los Angeleno resides, and that even now keep me wondering from second to second whether I am living in heaven or hell.

This sense that appearances are deceiving, that a level of reality exists beyond anything my senses could observe, was a recurring theme. The woman with jungle-red nails and stiletto heels turned out to sing in the church choir, the teenager on the bus bench with a serpent tattooed on her neck was bringing soup to her grandmother, the black guy who looked like a pimp was a hospice nurse, the Vietnamese guy who looked like a hospice nurse was a crack dealer. South Central (as it was known back then), which I had always pictured as a bombed-out crater surrounded by razor wire, consisted largely of quiet residential streets lined with charming bungalows. After a couple of years, we moved to a gorgeous French Normandie courtyard apartment in the middle of insanely crowded Koreatown: a neighborhood so full of mesmerizing contradictions that it would be another eighteen years before I'd move again.

I've learned over the years not to let quiet residential streets and bird-of-paradise bushes lull me into a false sense of security. But I've also learned that the opposite of security is not necessarily danger: it's risk, letting go, opening up to the city's vaunted, and entirely merited, sense of possibility. As I crawl in a sea of 101 freeway traffic on a Friday afternoon, quiver like an atom in the molecule of a packed Hollywood Bowl, tilt through the noxious brown sky on a return flight into LAX—peering out the airplane window stunned to think that somewhere in that endless, dun-colored grid are my apartment, my bed, my toothbrush—questions like these rise constantly to mind: Isn't it by the merest chance that in this chaotic megapolis I've somehow managed to find a place to live, my way as a writer, friends who can stand me? Isn't it at least a minor miracle that the vast majority of us get through any given day without being hit by a car, shot by a stray bullet, or struck by a toppling palm tree? Isn't it only a short step from there—the consistent avoidance of the cataclysmically bad—to the notion that it is just as likely that a stroke of *good* fortune will soon come one's way?

Living so close to Hollywood doesn't hurt this line of thinking. Inch for inch, LA has to have some of the most beautiful people on earth: security guards who look like Errol Flynn, carwash cashiers built like Marilyn Monroe. The cornucopia of cultures, the gorgeous weather, the overflowing farmer's markets combine at times to impart an almost ludicrous sense of abundance.

But, as with every other good thing in life, there's a downside, too. I still dream of New England: the fields of cows, the old barns, the lilacs in spring.

But nowadays when I go back, I can't help myself. *Everything's so small,* I think sadly. *Everyone's so fat.*

ZUPPA ALLA CANAVESANA: GRILLED BREAD AND CABBAGE SOUP WITH CRUNCHY CHEESE CRUST

Adapted from *Celebrating Italy*, by Carol Field

This recipe comes by way of my landscape architect/garden designer friend Judy M. Horton. Judy is an expert in all things Southern Cal, especially flora, and has long been associated with garden conservancies and organizations throughout the state. A visit means the blessed respite of sitting in the shade of her gorgeous garden, nibbling cheese and grapes, drinking tea while butterflies flit, bees drone, birds build nests, and we solve the problems of the world. Afterwards, she always gives me a tour, pointing out, say, the rare yellow clivia, the bank of potted hydrangeas descended from a single cutting nabbed (with permission) from the bud vase on a restaurant table, the Buddha's hand, aka "fingered citron," a tree bearing fragrant, compellingly claw-shaped citrus.

Many years ag, several of us gals were having a potluck and Judy brought this casserole. Meaty broth, sausages, bread, cheese: what's not to like? The pinch of cloves brings the whole thing alive. And for any mingy calorie counters, don't stint on life! Have a big helping, then clean up the kitchen, sweep the floors, bring out the garbage, and take a long, observant stroll around the streets of your 'hood.

INGREDIENTS

1 pound savoy cabbage
4 cloves garlic
½ cup butter or ¼ cup butter and ¼ cup olive oil
8 slices stale country bread
2 pounds onions, thinly sliced
Salt
1 ¼ cups meat broth
4–6 Italian sausages
⅓ pound (or more) strong, well-aged fontina or toma cheese, shredded
¼ cup parmesan cheese, plus additional as needed
Pepper
Large pinch ground cloves

TO PREPARE

1. Parboil the cabbage leaves 1–2 minutes, drain, and dry. Peel and flatten the garlic with the side of a cleaver. Melt 5 tablespoons butter in a small heavy skillet and add the garlic. Dip the slices of country bread into this mixture and sauté over medium heat until they are lightly toasted. Alternatively, brush the slices with the butter-garlic mixture and bake them in a 375-degree oven until golden and dried out, about 20 minutes.
2. Warm 3 tablespoons butter in a heavy-bottomed casserole, add the onions and salt, and cook over very low heat 45–60 minutes, stirring occasionally. The cooked onions will be reduced in quantity and invitingly browned; stir in the broth and scrape up any stray bits that have stuck to the bottom of the pan. After 45 minutes, prick the sausages with a fork and add to the onions. Cover and continue cooking for 15 minutes. Mix together the fontina and parmesan cheeses.
3. Cut the sausage into 3 or 4 pieces. In a high-sided earthenware tureen or glass casserole, make a layer of cabbage leaves, strew several pieces of sausage on top, then put on a layer of bread over them and season with grindings of fresh pepper and a sprinkling of ground cloves. Sprinkle

additional parmesan cheese lightly over the top. Bathe the layers with a couple of ladlefuls of broth and onions. Continue the layering process until you have used up all the ingredients. Finish with the combined cheeses, then add the final ladlefuls of broth.

4. Heat the oven to 375 degrees. Bake until the broth has been mostly absorbed and the cheese on top has formed a golden crust, at least 2 hours. The trick is to be careful that the crust doesn't burn or get brown too quickly; if you find that it has, set a piece of foil over the top of the baking dish.

5. Serve the soup in warm bowls, being sure to divide the crusty cheese topping among them.

6. Everyone's so thin!

⇒ 8 ⇐

My Mercifully Brief Life as a Lawyer

From approximately 1990 to 1994, I worked as a lawyer in Los Angeles. I'd lived in a world that was one kind of lie as a drunk, and as a lawyer, I lived in a world that was a different—in a way, a worse—lie. The drunk is at least willing to die for what he believes in. The drunk is willing to pay the consequences of his bondage.

I refrained from personalizing my office, on the theory that the less homey I made it, the easier it would be to bolt when the time came. I finally did bolt—and I have never, for one second, looked back.

I did, however, get freelance work doing legal research and writing for a plaintiff's employment discrimination firm that supported me during the first ten or so years of my apprenticeship as a creative writer. That whole time, I never quite made the jump to online legal research. I much preferred the law library: tracking down the tan books, with their red and black bindings, lugging them back to my seat, spreading them out, piling them into teetering stacks, quietly and with excitement building a well-reasoned argument.

I never looked back, but I've never regretted those years of freelancing. They taught me patience, perseverance, gratitude, long-suffering, and, above all, how to abide. I wrote the below in the mid– to late '90s.

My first book was published in 2005.

◊ ◊ ◊ ◊

I still support myself with occasional legal research and writing, and at the downtown LA Law Library, I still keep one eye on my books and the other on actual human beings. Something about law libraries attracts oddballs: sad, grubby types with messy piles of old, smudged-up notebooks. One old guy, yellowing hair neatly combed, shabby suit hanging from his skeletal frame, *sits in the exact same spot in the exact same position*—head bowed over a book whose pages he *never turns*—ALL DAY LONG. Once, I saw him go into the bathroom, but other than that, he never moves. The librarian tells me he used to practice law, snapped somehow, and has been coming to the library every day for the past nine years. Another man has long, wild hair and a beard, wears a filthy rust-colored pullover, and writes on a legal pad, line after line, page after page—not words, but squiggles, like the waves children draw—ALL DAY LONG.

My heart breaks to imagine the burning passion they must have to figure out the rules, to learn the answers, to get, once and for all, at HOW THINGS WORK. If only they turn enough tissue-thin pages, write down enough volume and page numbers, stare long enough at some fiendishly unintelligible index, they must think, someday they will figure it all out.

I know exactly how they feel: I am still trying to figure it out, too. I will always instinctively side with almost any plaintiff over any corporate defendant, any employee over any employer, any member of a minority over any alleged bigot, but these days I do not delude myself that my legal work even remotely promotes racial harmony or sexual tolerance. I know too much about my own capacity for hatred, my own propensity to hold on to the compulsions and resentments that are killing me, to believe that a lawsuit could heal those kind of wounds in anyone else.

Could it be, I wonder more and more, that what we really need is not to arm ourselves with more lawyers, but to look into each other's eyes, to grasp each other's fragile hands, to crack a joke, because, if only for a second, we have glimpsed another suffering human being as desperately in need of help as ourselves? Could it be, as Amos Oz has theorized, that a sense of humor is the last bulwark against fanaticism, and that therefore the worst thing about the legal world is that it lacks a sense of humor? Does William Rehnquist know any more about how the world really works than the wild-haired man writing squiggles on his legal pad all day?

Sitting in the library, surrounded by my highlighters and Post-its and *Federal Reporters*, I don't have those kinds of answers. In the end, we are all like the people in my old torts textbook: the aunt who had the chair pulled out from beneath her without warning, the fat lady in the grocery store insulted for no good reason, the beautiful girl maimed by a face-ful of lye. In the end, we go through life assaulted at random, blindsided by tragedy, stumbling through the dark night and occasional lights of a mysterious world. We are good at finding people to blame, but the flashes of light, the rare moments of illuminating grace in which we are given to see how often our suffering is self-imposed: who, I keep wondering, is responsible for those?

"The light shines in darkness and the darkness has not understood it." I know a little bit more now than I used to, but none of it has come from a law book.

PAD THAI PESTO

From the law library, I'd sometimes walk down Broadway to Chinatown. LA's Chinatown is far from the most authentic 'hood in which to sample Thai (or hardly any other Asian) food in LA: we have Little Tokyo, the Sawtelle District, and practically the entire cities of Garden Grove, Monterey, Rosemead, and Alhambra, among others, for that. Still, I'd go to Pho 69 for vermicelli with shrimp paste, charred pork, and egg rolls, or to ABC Seafood for dim sum, or to the 99 Ranch Market for packages of scallion pancakes and frozen dumplings.

Thai basil has long, narrow, purplish leaves, a purple flower, and a pleasingly sharp, faintly licorice taste. Along with dried shrimp powder, red chile with garlic paste, Thai fish sauce, roasted peanuts, fresh limes, and an array of dried noodles, it can be found for mere pennies at any decent Thai or Asian market.

I don't know how "authentic" this is, but it takes about three minutes to make and is addictively delicious.

INGREDIENTS

1 cup Thai basil
2 cloves of smashed garlic
1 teaspoon dried shrimp powder
2 teaspoons red chile with garlic paste

1 tablespoon Thai fish sauce
1 teaspoon sugar
1 tablespoon roasted peanuts
¼ teaspoon pepper
¼ cup canola or peanut oil
Juice of 1 lime

TO PREPARE

1. In a blender or food processor, combine the ingredients.
2. Pulse until blended and mixture is relatively smooth. Serve with rice, egg, or shrimp noodles.

⇒ 9 ⇐

Notes on a Soup Kitchen

Reading Dostoevsky's *The Brothers Karamazov*, what resonates most deeply isn't Ivan's hatred of evil, or Alyosha's unflagging goodness, or the cruel death of little Ilusha. No, the passage where I really think—"That's me"—is spoken by an acquaintance of Father Zossima's, a doctor, "a man getting on in years, and undoubtedly clever."

> The more I love humanity in general, the less I love man in particular. In my dreams, I often make plans for the service of humanity, and perhaps I might actually face crucifixion if it were suddenly necessary. Yet I am incapable of living in the same room with anyone for two days together. I know from experience. As soon as anyone is near me, his personality disturbs me and restricts my freedom. In twenty-four hours I begin to hate the best of men: one because he's too long over his dinner, another because he has a cold and keeps on blowing his nose. I become hostile to people the moment they come close to me. But it has always happened that the more I hate men individually the more I love humanity.

I experienced this phenomenon myself recently when a fellow parishioner interrupted my pre-Mass prayer for the prisoners on death row by asking me to move so he could reach his seat. The nerve, bothering *me,* when there were other, empty pews! The crass insensibility, the swinish lack of consideration, the vulgar, ill-bred boor!

Thus, one morning a week, I volunteer at the LA Catholic Worker's Skid Row soup kitchen: not because I love mankind so much, but because I don't. As you may know, the Catholic Worker is a lay movement started by Dorothy Day and Peter Maurin in the 1930's that espouses hospitality to the poor, social justice, and "voluntary poverty." Everything about the setup at the kitchen goes against my grain: it's not work itself I mind, but *team*work, taking direction, small talk with strangers, the whole unfamiliar situation in which I'm expected, on some level, to "perform."

That's how I felt at first anyway. The fact is I didn't quite know what to expect and that always makes me nervous. I'd read Dorothy Day— *Loaves and Fishes*; *The Long Loneliness*—but I had no idea what "Catholic Workers" would be like in the flesh. Would they reject me since I still paid income tax, or shun me for owning a car? I mentally spruced up my spiritual CV, and imagined long, desultory conversations over the stove. What happened instead was I got a big, open-armed welcome and in about two minutes they had me buttering bread and chopping celery so fast my head swam.

Getting personal information out of these folks was like pulling hen's teeth. I once asked Jeff Dietrich, a twenty-five-year veteran of the Worker, how he was doing. "Everything's going great!" he said. "Can't complain, same old, same old." The next day I read in their in-house newspaper, the *Catholic Agitator*, that he'd just finished a three-week fast in federal prison after having been arrested for cutting the fence at a Nevada nuclear testing site.

The kitchen itself is light and airy, and Catherine, Jeff's wife and another long-term member, has transformed the courtyard into a garden bower that would put the Junior League to shame. Picnic tables are shaded by flowering trees, a fountain gently plashes, parakeets warble from a huge birdcage. As for my "credentials," I soon figured out that the members of the Catholic Worker were way too busy serving the hungry, sheltering the homeless and caring for the dying in hospice—all in return for a weekly allowance of ten dollars apiece—to care whether I'd pulled up to the kitchen in a Rolls-Royce or hitchhiked.

My main job is serving salad, one long-handled serving spoonful per plate, and it's amazing how many variations on this simple theme our guests, as we call them, manage to come up with. One likes her salad dry from the top of the tub, another prefers runny from the bottom; they want it with extra tomatoes, no cabbage, on a separate plate, mixed with the beans, an extra serving, an extra-small serving. "Special orders don't upset *us!*" I mutter, and Bob, a fellow volunteer who dishes up beans, murmurs, "Funny, I always heard beggars *couldn't* be choosers."

Once the line starts rolling at 9:30, a raucous pageant begins, the contestants as unique as snowflakes. The hair alone is a jubilee: masses clotted like the roots of potbound plants, snake-thick dreadlocks, flaming hennaed aureolas, hair the texture of fiberglass insulation, hair with swirls and dips and glides enough to ski on, an Afro rioting two feet off its owner's head with a little white hankie draped on top, like a napkin on a bowl of fruit. I see fingernails as thick and horny as horse hooves; teeth like cracked corn, curved like tusks, and long as piano keys; lower gums with only two teeth left, one at each end, like goalposts. A tattoo in spidery cursive script on one man's neck reads, "I'm your puppet." Others, of naked women and Madonnas, are so crudely drawn they could have been outlined with icepicks.

In the Beverly Hills law office where I worked for four years, we rarely made eye contact: we couldn't bear to see our own emotions mirrored back from the very faces we each held responsible for our hatred and fear and defeat. Here at the kitchen, the guests let me look at them and, across the pot of beans, the bin of salad, the basket of bread, I let them look at me. In the course of a morning, I look into hundreds of pairs of eyes, say "Hey, what's up, pintos today!" or "There you go, careful now, it's hot!" or "Good morning!" *What's so fucking good about it?* some of them ask.

A kind of hypnotic rhythm sets in as the cardboard plates, white as hosts, are passed hand over hand, one by one, minute after minute, for two and a half hours as the line keeps coming on strong. By eleven o'clock, our backs ache from standing in one spot on the concrete floor. "Cripples for Christ!" I remark to Bob. "He keeps me runnin'!" Bob replies. *Me, too,* I think, though I'm not quite sure where.

For a while, I reveled in the starry-eyed realization that we weren't serving the poor; they were serving us! And while that may be true on some level, the fact is nothing could be clearer than that we are serving them and that most of them couldn't serve us even if they wanted to, and it's a pretty good bet they don't. On our side of the line, we have relatively pleasing personalities, clothes that fit, sound teeth. Our fingernails are clipped, our hair is cut, our zippers zip. We have things to put on a resumé and all our limbs. We wear both shoes.

What may shed more light than trying to figure out who is serving whom, is to recognize that we are all, in our own ways, looking for help. It may be simplistic to say that they are asking for food for their bodies, while we are seeking food for our souls. But to gloss over the distinction is to deny the difference between poverty—the grinding, crushing kind of poverty, imposed by our collective greed, that condemns people to expend every ounce of physical and psychic energy on locating the basic necessities of life—and the "voluntary" poverty espoused by Dorothy Day, ironically a kind of luxury open only to those for whom those basic necessities, by God's grace, have already been fulfilled.

One woman's shirt is so low-cut her nipples show; the next woman is swaddled in blankets, her feet wrapped in filthy strips of unraveling cloth, as if she were Lazarus emerging from the tomb. A T-shirt reads "At my age, sex is the last thing on my mind. It's the first thing, too." One man looks "normal": the next day I see him featured in a newspaper article about welfare cuts and discover he is schizophrenic with fourteen dollars a month in spending money, most of which goes for soap to assuage a disorder that compels him to obsessively launder his clothes.

Some of the guests never shut up and some of them won't talk at all. Some of them sing, some of them read, some say, "Lord be saved!" Some of them stink, and not the polite sweat you or I might work up after an hour at the gym: these are smells that conjure up caves and swamps and outdoor latrines. Some of them have breath like the moldy air from unplugged refrigerators; across the counter drift odors, penetrating as menthol, that should be emanating from the undersides of scrofulous wings instead of the shirts of human beings.

But while it looks to be clear that our side is a blessing, and theirs is a curse, sometimes you have to wonder. I think of the snowy-white shirts my lawyer boss used to wear—his tailor came to the office to fit him—with a raised white monogram over the breast pocket, thick, starched cuffs, and heavy gold cufflinks of crossed golf clubs. I think of his small plump hands, smooth as a girl's, the nails protected with a gloss of clear polish. At least I *think* those were his hands: the manicured hands and bespoke shirts, the silk ties and Italian loafers and the late-model Benzes blend together with all the other Benzes and Bally briefcases and Mont Blanc pens of all the other indistinguishable lawyers: the indistinguishable eyes with all the warmth of a combination lock; the sweat bred out of their pores until they smelled as bland and inoffensive as a plastic credit card.

That job constituted a kind of death that was as terrifying, in its way, as the prospect of starvation, and it is a measure of my own cowardice to say that quitting it—giving up the money—was the bravest thing I've ever done. My faith is so puny I imagined ending up a bag lady, one of those people I can love from a distance, out of pity, but after an hour bore and annoy me: one of those people on whose plate, come Thursday morning, I heap a mound of salad.

"But what can be done? What can one do in such a case? Must one despair?" asks Dostoevsky's doctor.

"No. It is enough that you are distressed. Do what you can and it will be reckoned unto you," replies Father Zossima.

I'm never sure I'm doing all I can. But I do know that Christ is where we all meet, whether we are in soup lines, or high, air-conditioned offices, or modest book-lined apartments. We are the hungry, the greedy, the doubters; all of us fallen; all of us aching, whether we know it or not, to be redeemed. Christ is here in the brilliant cascades of bougainvillea, the bright parakeets' song, in the donated food; in the members of the Catholic Worker who serve the poor not one morning per week, but seven days and nights; in us volunteers, in the salad, the spoon, in my hand that offers, the hands that accept.

I am here not because my being here will make a difference, but because it very well may not.

I am here because Christ said, "As you have done unto the least of these brothers of mine, so have you done unto me."

I am here because every so often, as I pass the white plates, one of my fingers touches one of theirs.

FLAGEOLETS GRATIN

Adapted from *Sunday Suppers at Lucques* by Suzanne Goin

I once invited a couple of members of the LA Catholic Worker to dinner. I really wanted to make things nice for them. I decided on cassoulet for a main dish and labored all day: the side dishes, the salad, the dessert.

I brought the cassoulet out steaming. I held the dish aloft so it could be admired from all angles. I set it down on the table and spooned out the first luscious serving. My guests looked up, clearly trying hard to look enthusiastic. I'd forgotten about the meal they served up three days a week. "Oh," one of them said finally. "Beans?"

Lucques is a restaurant in West Hollywood owned and operated by chef Suzanne Goin. Flageolets are a fancy French shell bean, sometimes known as the caviar of beans, pale celadon in color and with a subtle, borderline nutty flavor. Ordinarily I wouldn't dream of coughing up seven bucks for a bag of dried beans—but last December I splurged at Bristol Farms and made this for Christmas dinner.

INGREDIENTS

1 ½ cups dried flageolet beans
4 tablespoons extra-virgin olive oil
1 large bulb fennel, sliced into ¼-inch slices
2 Vidalia or other sweet onions, thinly sliced, about 3–4 cups of sliced onion
2 teaspoons fresh thyme
1 tablespoon butter
Kosher salt or fleur de sel
Coarsely ground black pepper

TO PREPARE

1. Rinse and wash flageolet beans. Cover with water and soak beans for up to 8 hours. Pour beans and soaking water into a heavy-bottomed pot, adding water if necessary to cover beans by 3 inches with water, and bring to a simmer. Cook for one hour and add 2 teaspoons or so of kosher salt. Cook for another half hour and taste. Continue cooking until beans are cooked through and have lost their raw, coarse taste. Take care not to overcook, as flageolet beans turn to mush quickly. Beans can be cooked two days ahead of time and stored, in their cooking water, in the refrigerator.

2. Preheat oven to 400. Toss fennel slices with 1 tablespoon of olive oil in a large bowl. Spread fennel on a baking sheet and roast until golden brown, about 20 minutes. Remove from oven and set aside. Raise heat to 425.

3. Meanwhile, in a large ovenproof casserole (large enough to hold the finished gratin) or sauté pan, warm the olive oil and the sliced onion over high heat. Add 1 teaspoon of kosher salt and 1 teaspoon of thyme and some freshly ground pepper. Cook for 6 minutes, stirring often. Reduce heat to medium, and add 1 tablespoon of the butter. Cook for another 15 minutes, stirring often. Onions will start to caramelize. Then turn the heat to low and cook for 10 more minutes until the onions are a deep caramel-brown color. Remove from heat.

4. Suzanne goes a whole step further, involving what to me sounded like a huge load of breadcrumbs, more butter, more thyme, and cooking the whole thing in the oven.

5. I made it her way once and for sure it was good but I felt way too heavy on the breadcrumbs. (She called for two cups and the problem may have been I didn't make them from scratch but used Progresso). Anyway, the point is that I had some cooked beans left over that I'd stuck in the fridge with a bit of leftover caramelized onion. And when I heated them together the next day I realized I actually liked that better than the finished dish that had required a bunch more work.

Nonetheless, if you want to do it her way...

THE ADDITIONAL INGREDIENTS

4 tablespoons butter
2 cups fresh breadcrumbs
Chopped flat-leaf parsley

AND THE ADDITIONAL INSTRUCTIONS

1. If you are using the pan you used to caramelize the onions to bake the gratin, set it aside. Otherwise, scrape onions into a gratin dish or earthenware baking dish and set aside.

2. In a medium bowl, toss the breadcrumbs with remaining 1 teaspoon of thyme and a handful of fresh chopped parsley. Melt the remaining 4 tablespoons of butter over medium heat. Cook for about 3 minutes, swirling the pan regularly until the butter browns and smells nutty—

but be careful, it will burn quickly from that point. Pour the butter over the breadcrumbs and toss thoroughly with a spoon.

3. Assemble the dish: combine the cooked beans and roasted fennel. Taste beans to make sure they are properly salted. Reserving cooking liquid from beans, strain the cooked beans and fennel and add to the gratin dish or casserole, spooning them carefully on top of the caramelized onions. The beans should only come three-quarters up the side of the dish, as they will continue to expand during cooking. Then, carefully pour in bean cooking liquid to come about a finger's width below the top of the beans. (The beans will cook and soak up this liquid during their baking time.) Cover the top of the dish with the buttered crumbs.

4. Place gratin in the 425-degree oven. Bake for 60–90 minutes, until gratin is bubbling and the breadcrumbs on top are deeply browned. Remove from oven and let the dish rest for 10 minutes before serving.

≫ 10 ≪

Smiles

When Gregor Samsa awoke one morning from troubled dreams he found himself transformed in his bed into a monstrous insect. He was lying on his hard shell-like back and by lifting his head a little he could see his curved brown belly, divided by stiff arching ribs, on top of which the bed-quilt was precariously poised and seemed about to slide off completely. His numerous legs, which were pathetically thin compared to the rest of his bulk, danced helplessly before his eyes.

"What has happened to me?" he thought. It was no dream.

—Franz Kafka, "The Metamorphosis"

Wednesday, Dr. Catalfo jabs and scrapes and probes, grinds down to a nub the next-to-the-last molar on the upper right hand side of my mouth and, at the end of two and a half hours, attaches a temporary crown. The whole area is raw the next day, and the day after that the tooth itself starts aching, a bright bulb of pain burning down to the root.

I hate to be a whiner, but Saturday I reluctantly show up at the clinic, write "Emergency" under "Reason for Visit" and hang around for two hours waiting for Dr. Catalfo to squeeze me in between regular patients. He is young enough to be my son, with healthy gums and sparkling white teeth that light up his whole handsome face like a movie marquee. After a five-second inspection of my mouth, he prescribes ibuprofen and warm-water-and-salt rinses. "It seems to be a little deeper than that," I offer lamely, but of course the doctor knows best. I obediently return home and follow his directions.

Sunday, one of the teeth in my lower jaw starts throbbing too, a deep, razor-like pain that slashes right through the flimsy barrier thrown up by aspirin. Then the tooth to the rear of the one with the temporary crown starts aching, and next, the one in front of it. Great, I think grimly, my whole mouth is rotting. I reconnoiter by pressing a series of toothpicks against the gum line, but the locus of the pain keeps moving. One minute, it seems to be an upper molar; the next, a lower incisor. By Monday, my whole right jaw is humming with the kind of pain that registers on your consciousness as a pulsing wash of red and I'm gulping down six or eight ibuprofen at a whack. I eye my husband's tool box, seriously considering wrenching out the offending tooth with a pair of pliers. Instead, I suppress the fear that Dr. Catalfo will think me a nuisance and show up again Tuesday morning.

After signing in with the receptionist—a bored twenty-year-old with scarlet talons and lips outlined in black—I try to settle down in the waiting room. My fellow patients gazing balefully at the floor, like mourners at a funeral, and the corporate decor—dun-colored rug, cheap beige furniture, hidden speakers blaring, "Wake me up, before you go-go/Don't leave me hangin' on-n, like a yo-yo"—make me feel edgy and disoriented.

I have spent a lifetime waiting in rooms like this. I have had cavities filled and abscesses drained and impacted wisdom teeth pulled. I have had my gums cut, scraped, scaled and sutured. I have had adult orthodontia, so many root canals I've lost count, thousand-dollar crowns that had to be done over a few months later. I have had so many X-rays taken that I long ago resigned myself to dying of radium poisoning.

None of this has done much good. In spite of all my efforts, my teeth are still so sensitive to heat and cold that I have to cradle every sip of coffee and bite of ice cream on my tongue like pablum before swallowing. Soft teeth run in my family, and I religiously brush and floss, but I have never seen these as factors mitigating my failure. My mouth is the Sisyphean emblem that no matter how hard I try, no matter how much pain I withstand, no matter how much money I pay, I will never be clean enough, pretty enough, perfect enough.

I put my purse under the chair, sigh, and open my book—*Kafka: The*

Complete Stories—to "The Metamorphosis." I'd remembered it as a coolly detached tale of existential alienation but, at thirty years' remove from the first read, I am struck instead by its tenderness, its almost religious overtones. Now I see the apple, launched in disgust by Gregor's father to lodge in his shattered carapace, as a symbol of man's ejection from the Garden of Eden. Now I, too, have experienced the way that, when it comes to passion, transformation often feels so unsettlingly close to deformation: "Was he an animal, that music had such an effect on him?" Approaching middle age, now I am beginning to grasp one of the terrible truths of "The Metamorphosis": that I live, in one way, because so many other people have died—and that my turn is coming, too.

Gregor's heartrending deterioration and death paradoxically free his family to again live a "normal" life, and the ending, when his vacationing sister springs to her feet in joy and stretches "her young body," is both genius and chilling. I want to go over it again but, sitting in this nondescript waiting room, concentrating is difficult. I am not sure whether life is imitating art or art is imitating life. All I know is that across the room a large woman with frizzy red hair is slumping further and further down in her seat, as if she would like to get up and run but can't because her bones are dissolving.

"Help me," she moans loudly. "Somebody please help me."

"Excuse me," I say politely, catching the receptionist's eye, "but this woman needs assistance."

"Her appointment's at nine," the receptionist snaps, biting down on a glazed donut. "The doctor will call her when he's ready."

"I think I'm going to throw up," the woman groans. An elderly Korean man sitting to her left gets up and moves. I look to the receptionist again, but she has turned her back, a phone glued to her ear. I walk over to the woman, perch gingerly on the seat beside her, and take hold of one of her clammy hands.

"You're going to be fine," I say stiffly, giving her an awkward pat on the back.

"I didn't sleep last night!" she wails. "I didn't sleep!"

"You can sleep as soon as you get home," I tell her. "The dentist will be here any minute."

"I'm so *tired*," she gasps. She wriggles further down in her seat, a lapless worm in a denim skirt but, somehow, I sense she is glad to have me nearby. We sit holding hands, in miserable, companionable silence. Her flesh is hot and damp, repugnant yet strangely familiar. When the dentist comes in, takes her elbow and leads her away, the waiting room seems lonelier than ever.

Finally, a ponytailed teenager in a blue smock leads me down the hall to the last room on the left. I hang my purse on a peg by the door, beside a black baseball cap, its bill coated faintly with dust. I picture its owner walking blindly out the door, the hand that would have otherwise reached for the forgotten cap laid gently over his bleeding mouth. My own mouth is killing me, its insistent, sickly throb like the beat of a drum. After lowering myself into the vinyl recliner, I study the Seurat print, a tableau of ladies in bustles promenading with their parasols, mounted on the mauve wall. Instead of calming me down, this nakedly manipulative ploy deepens my agitation yet further. Given the setting, this is art that lies, as misleading as the dental insurance plan I once joined called Smiles. I would have more faith in the integrity of the profession if I were gazing instead at Munch's *The Scream*.

After another fifteen minutes, Dr. Catalfo appears, dressed in his usual outfit: rubber gloves, green earplugs, and a plastic visor that descends over his healthily tanned face like the windshield of a motorcycle. He's clearly in a hurry. I imagine his waiting patients laid out helplessly in other rooms, their jaws numb, staring blankly at their own blurry prints of enervated water lilies and pastel haystacks.

"Still having a little pain?" he asks.

"More than a little," I say with uncharacteristic firmness. "I think something's wrong with one or two of my lower teeth, too."

"That's a common phenomenon," Dr. Catalfo chuckles. "When one tooth hurts, it often sends pain impulses to the surrounding teeth. We call it 'sympathetic pain.'"

While I reflect that a pain that snakes itself into places that do not even technically hurt is anything but "sympathetic," he probes the gum with what feels like a sewing needle and I come halfway off the chair.

"Tender, is it?" he muses.

I grope for the words to communicate just how tender it is, but the part of my brain where that particular vocabulary would otherwise be stored is slack from a lifetime of disuse. "Something's wrong," is the best I can muster.

"Have you been rinsing with salt and warm water?" he asks briskly.

"Yes," I falter, "but..."

"I'm going to write a prescription for 600-milligram Motrin," he says, whipping out his pad, "and if that doesn't help, you can come back in and we'll take a look underneath."

Something surges through me like a current, a thin wire of anger at my insistence, so deeply ingrained I am not even sure where it comes from, on politely hanging back, on letting everyone else go first, on remembering that I am the least important person in the room.

"But this is my second time here already," I say. "Something's wrong. Can't you look underneath now?"

He hesitates a second, then sighs. "All right then, the other patients will just have to wait. Open."

With a tug from an instrument that looks like a pair of nail scissors, the lumpy porcelain shell slips off easily. Whatever lies beneath is raw nerve: exposing it to the open air results in a jolt of pain so sharp I salivate. My tongue moves instinctively to protect the afflicted area, the way you might lay a warm blanket over a frostbitten friend.

"I see what the problem is," says Dr. Catalfo, peering in. "We just need to cushion it a bit more. Go on," he urges, placing a white plastic mirror into my hand. "Take a look."

My eyes travel slowly, involuntarily to the site. From a patch of inflamed gum rises a lonely cylindrical nub, black as a volcano, rimmed with a moat of bright red blood. I think with a pang of Gregor Samsa's dumb endurance in the face of his alien, decaying body. What is the appropriate response to such a sight? Horror? Shame? Compassion? I close my eyes and say nothing and, after a minute, Dr. Catalfo takes the mirror away.

Humming to himself, he grinds down one side of the temporary, then applies a liquid that tastes like battery acid to the throbbing stub. Even the brush of a Q-tip hurts so much I am afraid I am going to start grunting, hyperventilating into the pain like a woman going into labor.

Then he says, "Open" again, aims a silver nozzle and blasts the tooth with one, two, three jets of dry, ice-cold air and the pain is so fierce—I didn't think it was legal for one person to inflict this kind of pain on another— that I break. I do what I have never in forty-five years allowed myself to do in a dentist's chair: I cover my crumpled face with my hands and burst into tears.

My first instinct is to apologize, to ensure that Dr. Catalfo does not experience a single moment of discomfort thinking that I blame him, and not myself, for this ghastly breach of etiquette. "I'm sorry," I sniffle, rocking back and forth, "I'm sorry, it just hurts so much."

◊ ◊ ◊ ◊

A corridor clears itself in my mind and I am walking toward another time, another dentist. I am eight years old, back with my mother in Portsmouth, New Hampshire, in the waiting room of Dr. Richardson, our family dentist. Dr. Richardson's office is in a gray Victorian with a gambrel roof and stained glass around the front door. In the waiting room, old issues of *Highlights* are lined up in martial rows on the coffee table, a nest of fake logs crouches in the cold fireplace and, in one corner, the dusty green spears of a sansevieria rise up, a bouquet of blades. Near the window in a bubbling aquarium, fish of jungle red and tropical blue slash the murky water. I stand with my nose pressed against the glass watching them swim mutely back and forth, their eyes fathomless pinpricks, and try not to think about what lies on the other side of the office door.

After a few minutes, the nurse, in cat's-eye glasses and starched cap, ushers me in. She smiles stiffly, her mouth a red slash, and helps me into the black leather chair with its padded armrests. An amethyst lamp burns overhead, water flows into a miniature sink and, on a round glass tray whose white edges are fluted like a piecrust, the sterile instruments glint like knives: the tilted mirror that exposes every millimeter of my mouth to Dr. Richardson's piercing gaze, the hooked picks, the pointed probers. Only one thing is missing: a syringe. My brothers and sisters and I have our teeth drilled without anesthetic.

Dr. Richardson glides in, wearing a white, short-sleeved tunic that buttons up the side, and performs a quick examination. The chemical smell of alcohol clings to his ungloved fingers, which probe my mouth like sausages.

"We'll do three today," he nods to the nurse, extracting the drill, heavy as a padlock, from its stand. As a sound like a cement mixer fills the room, my body stiffens, my sweating palms start to slide on the slick armrests and my fingers—even at that age-I bite my nails raw—form rigid claws. I descend into a kind of trance, willing myself to endure, as porcelain, old fillings, and what feels like the occasional chunk of bone are reduced to rubble with agonizing slowness and sucked by the nurse down a gurgling tube.

"I can stand this second, I can stand this second," I repeat to myself like a mantra. When the pain becomes particularly intense, the buzzing whine seems to segue into a higher pitch, a waa-waa-waa, as if the drill itself were registering a protest.

After the session is over, Dr. Richardson takes me into the back room—a made-over pantry—and lets me choose a prize from a box of Disney animal erasers. I thank him profusely, like a wrongfully convicted prisoner who has finally been set free. Foolishly, I imagine that this time will be the last, that my body will stop betraying me, that if I bear up well enough, I won't have to come back again.

Many years later, I learned that on the East Coast in the '50s, many children had their teeth drilled without Novocaine: apparently, some residual Calvinistic doctrine held that children did not feel pain the same way adults did. At the time, however, I assumed my parents had decided that anesthesia was simply unnecessary, an extravagance. In our household, everything was an extravagance, including heat, normal food, and clothes like the rest of the world wore. Our bedrooms in winter were the temperature of meat lockers, we sometimes ate sandwiches made of spaghetti or tartar sauce, and my mother, to cite just one example, had sewn herself a bathing suit out of leftover upholstery fabric that was so heavy she would have drowned if she had ever tried to actually swim in it. Not that there was much chance of that. It was only four miles to the beach, but we hardly ever went: we couldn't spare the gas.

Over the years, my siblings and I and even my parents turned all this into a joke, but it was always a joke steeped in shadow. Economizing is one thing, but this was frugality edged with panic, the reflection of belief in a universe that was anything but loving, anything but accommodating, anything but abundant. It was not that my mother and father lacked love. We just happened to be the latest in a long line of people who felt the same anxiety and fear and inability to cope that we did and, like us, had never found a way to talk about it: my maternal grandmother, the daughter of an alcoholic, a hermit who went weeks without speaking a word and wore a path walking solitary circles around her Rhode Island farmhouse; Cousin Betsy, with her purse full of vodka nips, her splotched face and shaking hands, her seizures; Uncle Frank, his breath boozy with Ballantine Ale and Pall Malls, the town drunk who died of cirrhosis.

I suppose it was no surprise that somewhere along the line I began to look forward, in a queasy, adrenaline-charged way, to the dentist's chair, began to take a kind of perverse pride in my ability to withstand both physical and emotional pain, began to crave the ersatz feeling of control that comes from hiding it. Somewhere along the line, I lost twenty years of my own life to drinking, Prometheus chained to a rock gnawing out my own liver.

I no longer drink, but I have come to see that my craving for alcohol was only a symptom of something deeper that I have never been able to quite identify or heal. A grown woman, I still wage a daily struggle with the psyche of an eight-year-old. If I smile, can I have the rubber Goofy? If I don't cry, will you like me? The simplest exchanges are tainted with this stupid, stubborn desire to please, this terror of exposing my true self.

◊ ◊ ◊ ◊

Then I am back in the chair and Dr. Catalfo is wiping my tears with the edge of the green bib and saying, "No, no, I'm the one who should be sorry. I didn't realize how sensitive it was."

True to form, I call myself a crybaby and crack a couple of jokes. Dr. Catalfo re-cements the temporary and writes out a prescription for Tylenol with codeine. "Don't forget your book," he calls as I turn to leave. As I pick it up from the counter, Kafka's odd, angular face peers enigmatically up from the cover.

Out in the sunlight, I study the photo closely. No matter how long I look, which way I turn it, I cannot quite decide whether the expression playing around the corners of his mouth is a smile—or a rictus of pain.

◊ ◊ ◊ ◊

Three weeks later, I go in and Dr. Catalfo installs the permanent crown. The process is painless and easy, a half-hour breeze. At the end, he inserts a piece of blue carbon paper between my jaws, instructs me to grind down and pronounces it a perfect fit.

"Here, take a look," he says, handing me the white, plastic mirror.

"Great match," I wisecrack. "Sort of an antique yellow, just like my other teeth." I am thinking that, in the end, perhaps making a joke of our collective suffering is as valid a solution as any other. Perhaps humor is the only sane response to a world that often seems so berserkly cruel. Perhaps, in the end, the truth of the human condition is so far beyond our ken that we are only capable of recognizing it as something comic and grotesque: Gregor Samsa turned into a giant cockroach, repulsive in one way—yet with the inviolable desire to love and be loved that enabled him to continue living his lonely, incomprehensible life.

As I climb out of the vinyl chair, Dr. Catalfo tilts my latest batch of X-rays to the light. "Just one more crown," he announces, tearing off a pink appointment slip. "Then, you'll be done," and his youthful voice is so assured that for a second I almost believe him.

CHEWY CHOCOLATE GINGERBREAD COOKIES

This is hands down my favorite cookie recipe. Making it is a bit of trouble, but the cookies have tooth, a rich, back-of-the-throat smoothness, and a complex bass note of cloves, nutmeg, and cocoa.

When you hit a mother-lode hunk of chocolate on top of all that, you'll know God really does love us.

And of course these are *super* good for your teeth.

INGREDIENTS

7 ounces of the best-quality semisweet chocolate you feel like splurging on
1½ cups plus 1 tablespoon all-purpose flour
1¼ teaspoons ground ginger
1 teaspoon ground cinnamon
¼ teaspoon ground cloves
¼ teaspoon ground nutmeg
1 tablespoon unsweetened cocoa powder
8 tablespoons (1 stick) unsalted butter
1 tablespoon freshly grated ginger
½ cup dark brown sugar, packed
¼ cup molasses
1 teaspoon baking soda
1½ teaspoons boiling water
¼ cup granulated sugar

TO PREPARE

1. Line two baking sheets with parchment. Chop chocolate into quarter inch chunks; set aside. In a medium bowl, sift together flour, ground ginger, cinnamon, cloves, nutmeg, and cocoa.

2. In the bowl of an electric mixer, fitted with the paddle attachment, beat butter and grated ginger until whitened, about 4 minutes. Add brown sugar; beat until combined. Add molasses; beat until combined.

3. In a small bowl, dissolve baking soda in 1½ teaspoons boiling water. Beat half of flour mixture into butter mixture. Beat in baking soda mixture, then remaining half of flour mixture. Mix in chocolate; turn out onto a piece of plastic wrap. Roll or pat batter to an inch or so thick, seal with plastic wrap, and refrigerate until firm (the recipe calls for 2 hours or more but, jammed for time, I've done 20 minutes and they've turned out fine).

4. Heat oven to 325 degrees. Roll dough into 1½-inch balls; place 2 inches apart on baking sheets. Refrigerate 20 minutes (again, I've skipped this part with no ill effect). Roll in granulated sugar. Bake until the surfaces crack slightly, 10–12 minutes. Let cool 5 minutes, then transfer to a wire rack to cool completely.

5. Or if you're like me, as soon as the chocolate has cooled down enough not to burn out the roof of your mouth, start scarfing.

≫ 11 ≪

Langer's Pastrami and My Friend Joan

Langer's is a Jewish delicatessen near downtown LA that, according to a 2002 *New Yorker* article by Nora Ephron, serves "the finest pastrami sandwich in the world." Everyone goes to Langer's: executives, street people, tourists. My friend Joan has waited on them all.

Here's an interview I did with Joan for NPR's *All Things Considered* in 2005. My producer, the great Sara Sarasohn, was in town and that afternoon we went to the corner of Alvarado (Joan calls it Alvaweirdo) and 7th with our sound equipment. We caught Joan at Langer's just as she was finishing her shift.

HEATHER: Joan is sixty years old and has worked at Langer's for eighteen years. Every Thursday and Friday morning, she rises in her studio apartment, sets out for the half-hour walk, and reports for the breakfast shift in her waitressing uniform: a white shirt and black pants.

JOAN: Right now I have three pairs. Two of them have bleach stains on them but I just take a Magic Marker and make it black. Why wouldn't a person just get a new pair of pants? I don't know. It just seems to me that if it's working don't buy another pair. And I had a zipper that was broken and no one knew because you can wear your apron over it.

HEATHER: Joan can seem scattered—or, as she puts it, "dispersed"—but she's a crackerjack waitress. If she's done it once, she's done it a thousand times: described the difference between a phosphate and an egg cream, corned beef and brisket, the eight kinds of bread.

JOAN: Egg, white, wheat, sourdough, rye, and then we have kaiser roll, onion roll and French roll. That's sixty-five cents extra for the french roll.

HEATHER: Langer's is part of Joan's world but it's not her whole world. Weekends, she visits her friend at an eating-disorder hospital. On her day off, she volunteers at a Vietnamese convent that runs a shelter for homeless women. Nights she takes English classes at LA City College. Three years ago, she squared her shoulders and made what seemed like a huge commitment to herself: she determined to take one course a semester.

JOAN: It was scary because I didn't know if I could do it or if I had it within me to do it. I've done waitressing for so many years and I needed to work my brain. And I just went.

HEATHER: Joan hadn't been to school in forty years. When she went in to be tested, they told her she'd have to start out *two* levels below everyone else. She was the oldest person in the class. She struggled for weeks over a three-page paper—she told me over the phone "by the end I was slumped over in the fetal position *drooling*"—and then she pushed the delete button without having first saved it.

JOAN: I did purchase a Dell computer. I asked this man, a customer, to help and I went over to his house and just told him order for me. A computer is like a relationship—if it's not good going in, it doesn't get better. And this Dell computer was like having a Corvette. I should have had a bicycle.

HEATHER: Joan's always had a unique way of expressing herself and, thrillingly for me, the computer also means she now sends email. Her messages begin "My One and Only," or "You Are All Good," or "Oh dear God it is hard Fear Fear." Being in school has widened her vocabulary, livened up her conversation, and increased her self-confidence.

JOAN: Oh Heather this is so exciting. I got a piece of paper in the mail and it said that I have made the part-time honor roll at LA City College. It sounds kind of funny and kind of like a joke but it is a big deal.

HEATHER: If you happen in on a Thursday or Friday, Joan will recommend the Number 19: pastrami, Swiss cheese, cole slaw, Russian dressing. It might be the finest pastrami sandwich in the world. But that still isn't the *best* thing about Langer's.

ASPARAGUS GLAZED WITH LEMON AND SOY SAUCE

A recipe with a mere four ingredients (not counting salt) is a thing of beauty. I always find asparagus faintly scary: a sophisticated vegetable that rarely comes canned or frozen. Unlike, say, carrots or potatoes, you can't, if all else fails, simply throw asparagus in a pot of boiling water, douse with salt and pepper, and still have a dish that doesn't make you feel shame.

No, asparagus requires a bit of finesse. This dish plays butter, soy sauce and lemon off each other in a glaze that perfectly complements those tender-crisp, emerald-green stalks.

INGREDIENTS

1 pound asparagus
Salt
1½ tablespoons butter
1½ tablespoons soy sauce
Juice of ½ lemon
Fresh black pepper

TO PREPARE

1. Wash and snap the stalks at the point where they naturally break. Cook in rapidly boiling water for 2–3 minutes, or until crispy-tender. Run under cold water and drain. Pat the stalks dry with a paper or cloth towel.
2. Melt the butter with the soy sauce, lemon juice and pepper in a sauté or frying pan and boil down to a (thrillingly) syrupy glaze. Add the asparagus and stir or shake the stalks around in the pan to ensure that all are coated with the glaze and thoroughly heated. Serve at once or eat straight out of the pan.

⇒ 12 ⇐

Milvio: Food for a Wake

Somewhere around 1994, I hooked up with the LA branch of the Catholic Worker: as I mentioned earlier, a lay movement started in New York City in the '30s by ex-Communist and Catholic convert Dorothy Day.

Over the years, I've volunteered at their soup kitchen, donated money, written articles for their newspaper. One night not long ago, I brought over a pan of coconut squares for their Wednesday night liturgy and potluck and found myself at a wake instead. Milvio, a guest in the house for the past year, had been murdered: shot to death in a Skid Row dispute over a twenty-dollar bill.

In the dining room, a crowd milled about and Milvio was laid out up front in a gray metal casket. I wasn't sure of the protocol so I didn't actually go over and look inside; I had a feeling you were supposed to wait until later.

I took one of the few remaining seats. Catherine, a no-nonsense ex-nun who has been a mainstay of the LA Catholic Worker for twenty-five years, began the service by lighting candles and incense. Then several people from the house spoke. Jeff—Catherine's husband, a rabble-rousing activist—noted that people on the street are often closer to God than "our middle-class friends." Sandy, a high school English teacher, observed that though poverty-stricken drug addicts like Milvio have never been the kind of success stories mainstream charities like to hold up as examples of why you should donate money to them, the Catholic Worker had considered it a privilege to shelter, feed, and clothe him.

This was all true enough in its way, but it was Martha—she'd recently spent seven months in jail for cutting the fence at a nuclear testing site—who provided the kind of human detail that made me feel a real pang at Milvio's passing. Martha told how she had always known that Milvio ironed his jeans, but could never figure out how he got the creases so sharp until one day, in his bedroom, she'd spotted a pan of something that looked like "old, old rice pudding," a kind of miracle, glue-like starch.

I ate my dinner—salad with ranch dressing, a leg of fried chicken—a few yards from the casket. Just before leaving, I finally went over to pay my respects. It's always unsettling to view a corpse. Everything was a few degrees off: the skin grayer than any real skin, the body in a box you never see a live person lying in. Even the parts you don't think of as much alive to begin with—eyelashes, fingernails—looked dead. A short, skinny braid snaked out from the part you couldn't see; the part where the bullet had gone through; that especially fragile spot on a human body—the back of the neck.

Milvio's murder was an illustration of the forces of darkness the members of the Catholic Worker so courageously picket against and go to jail for, but driving home that night, as the moon shone silver above the skyscrapers of downtown, I was not much thinking of the techno-corporate juggernaut of global economics or the contemptibility of my bourgeois life. What passed through my mind instead were odd little images I had flashed on during the service—Sandy's thumbnail, Eric's sideburns, the way Jeff rolls up the bottom of his shorts.

I thought of a God so tender that He numbers every hair on every head. I kept to the right, in the slow lane, and every so often my hand fluttered up to touch the back of my neck.

JEFF DIETRICH'S BREAD PUDDING
WITH WHISKEY SAUCE

Dorothy Day's followers don't call the places where they live with the poor "houses of hospitality" for nothing. Noone throws a party like the LA Catholic Worker. Thanksgiving, Seder, Our Lady of Guadalupe, your biopsy came back negative: they are *there*, with roast turkeys, giant pots of chili, pies galore, and plenty of booze.

I wrote the above piece a while ago. Jeff Dietrich, who's now been a member for forty years, is a crackerjack cook, with a talent for taking whatever's on hand (cartons of donated lemons, week-old bagels, crates of eggs) and coming up with a pot of something tasty, inventive, and crowd-worthy.

One signature dish is his bread pudding: eggy, a slightly crisped surface, and drenched with high-octane whiskey sauce.

When I asked if he'd part with the recipe, he responded with this email:

Bread pudding recipe with southern bourbon sauce, I like to pretend is a recipe from my southern grandmother, and while it tastes very similar to her bread pudding, it actually came from [community member] Martha who did a year of research and finally settled upon the recipe from The Joy of Cooking.

I have, as we all do, modified the recipe over the years, but the basic and excellent comes from The Joy of Cooking.

Ok—like all great recipes this one is simple AND BASIC.

BREAD PUDDING

INGREDIENTS

1½ pound loaf of french bread, sliced diagonally
1–2 cups of raisins inserted between the slices
1 quart milk (powdered milk or nonfat milk work fine)
2 cups sugar
3 tablespoons vanilla
4 tablespoons cinnamon
4 eggs

TO PREPARE

1. Place french bread slices in an appropriate-sized baking pan (a 9 x 12 inch baking pan or casserole would do nicely).

2. Insert raisins between the bread slices.
3. Mix together milk, sugar, vanilla, cinnamon, and eggs.
4. Pour mixture over bread slices. Cover and let soak for 1–10 hours.
5. Place in preheated oven at 350 degrees for 45 minutes to an hour.
6. The pudding should be firm and the bread should be crispy to slightly blackened. I like the crispy bread texture with the soft pudding.

WHISKEY SAUCE

This is the part that reminds me of my grandmother. It's an adult sauce so kids sometimes don't like it. It is basic sugar, butter, and whiskey.

INGREDIENTS

Whiskey, 2 tablespoons to ½ cup, depending on taste
½ pound butter
2 eggs
2 cups sugar
½ teaspoon salt
¼ teaspoon nutmeg

TO PREPARE

1. Melt butter and let cool.
2. Mix eggs, sugar, salt, nutmeg, and whiskey.
3. Add the mixture to the slightly cooled butter, turn the heat to low, and beat the hell out of It. The egg holds the whole thing together in a smooth, creamy, syrup-type sauce.
4. Pour a portion over the bread pudding to give it a glistening sheen. I sometimes just pour the entire mixture over the bread pudding because it is difficult to get your guests to understand that the sauce is the essential part of the recipe.

I have experimented with the milk and eggs to give a more puddingy texture. Also I am suggesting the maximum amount of whiskey because I like to knock people's socks off. You can substitute water for some of the whiskey. But the basic idea is the sharp smoky flavor combined with the sweetness of sugar and the smoothness of butter.
You can use the cheapest bourbon, brandy, or rum. No vodka or gin.

≫ 13 ≪

K-Town: Lost and Found

"Great problems are in the street," Nietzsche said, and as a writer, I not only need to get out and see that other folks are struggling, too, I need to get out, period. Koreatown is a melting pot—of cultures, races, demographics— and walking out the door into this heady mixture of the mundane and the exotic is stimulating stuff: the Armenian cobbler, the Cuban cigar store, the Vietnamese salon where Mai administers soothing pedicures.

As a Caucasian, I'm a minority in Koreatown, and if that gives me the solitude I need for my work, it also makes the moments of community seem that much more precious: I stop in so often at the Pio Pico library to pick up reserved books that the security guard once asked if I worked there; Crystal, the junkie who begs change outside the 7-Eleven, asks if I've had anything published lately; and, walking to Windsor Park in the cool of a winter dusk, I sometimes stop in at St. Gregory's and, along with the four or five elderly Korean parishioners scattered among the pews, kneel for a few minutes and pray.

Everything's within walking distance: one mango, two eggs, a handful of tomatoes at the corner produce truck, $2.99 bags of frozen pork dumplings at the Assi Supermarket, the strange little outdoor bazaar off Western, where for a week or so in early June, I always buy a pound of luscious, juicy cherries a day. Food—comfort, color, connection—is a major element of life in Koreatown. A stone's throw from the nondescript copy centers and anonymous dentist offices of the Wilshire corridor, there's Vim's for chow foon with shrimp and chinese broccoli, La Plancha for ninety-nine-cent pupusas, Kobawoo House for mung bean pancakes and kimchee. At the local 24 Hour Fitness, the air is thick with the smell of garlic.

Just when I know the neighborhood inside out, I discover someplace new: Liborio's Market, for a can of shredded coconut in syrup; the thrift store at the Commonwealth and 6th Congregational Church, where I once found a copy of *Onions in the Stew*, a book by one of my favorite writers, Betty MacDonald. There are adventures: the Sunday morning, for example, that Eloise, my friend Clam's eight-year-old daughter, drags us around the K-town Plaza *and* the K-town Galleria on a quest for a bubblegum cell phone. There are surprises: the morning I walk to the corner and find that overnight, the name of the closest cross street has been changed from 9th to James M. Wood. There is serendipity: a chamber music concert at St. Thomas the Apostle, from which I walk the dark streets home wrapped in the closing bars of Mozart's Flute Quartet in D Major.

Friday morning I walk to St. Basil's, where my friend Father Terry says eight o'clock Mass. Sipping a coffee outside the Serrano Starbucks afterwards, I watch the passing parade: tens of thousands of lives intersecting, then going off in their own directions; colliding, picking themselves up and gathering themselves to begin anew; the smallest act— the chance smile, the random act of rudeness—rippling out to our fellows in unseen ways.

I think of the parallel life that haunts the human psyche, the persistent suspicion that things would be better in some other place, if only we could find it. "Always you will arrive in this city," Constantine Cavafy wrote of his native Alexandria. "Do not hope for any other." For a minute I forget that I have responsibilities, work, a life. If I sit here another ten hours I'll be able to look west down Wilshire and, half a mile on, see the Romanesque tower of the United Methodist Church silhouetted against the rays of the setting sun.

I can never quite tell whether I'm losing myself or finding myself in Koreatown and I remember the exact day when I realized perhaps it didn't matter. That would be the afternoon I left my apartment to walk down San Marino and, through the window of a rundown tract house, heard the strains of the same Beethoven sonata I'd just finished playing on my own piano.

AUBERGE AT OJAI'S CHICKPEA FRITTERS AND FRISÉE

Ojai is a town an hour and a half northwest of LA full of olive groves, vineyards, luxury spas, and filthy rich former hippies. The charming downtown features a lovely shaded, sprawling park where, every summer, a classical music festival is held over a long weekend. You can get (cheap) lawn seats, bring a picnic, and eat under the live oaks. My ex-husband, Tim, and I did this often.

I never ate at Auberge at Ojai, which it appears is now closed, but I'm forever grateful for this recipe, which combines a deep-fried chickpea fritter (need I say more?) with a fresh, beautifully seasoned frisée salad.

Chickpea flour is readily available at any of the many mom-and-pop Indian stores in LA I treasure such visits, taking my time to survey the saffron yellow samosas in a display case under the heat light, the Mysore Sandal Soap and Dabur Herbal Toothpaste with Neem, the red lentils and basmati rice, the jars of cardamom pods, curry, coriander seeds, and garam masala.

Frisée, aka curly endive, as you may know, is a pale green, frilly lettuce. I live within walking distance of a 99 Cents Only Store where, among the bags of precut cabbage and mealy tomatoes, I have *found* frisée. I've also at various times found there whipping cream, parchment paper, fingerling potatoes, raspberries, blackberries, Toblerone white chocolate, Meyer lemons, Hass avocados, and fresh dill, tarragon, and basil. The problem is you never know.

Still, I love that my local dollar store sometimes carries the relatively exotic frisée. And I'm sure noone would arrest you if you substituted, say, spring mix.

CHICKPEA FRITTERS

INGREDIENTS

2 cups milk
2 tablespoons butter
½ teaspoon salt
⅛ teaspoon pepper
½ large garlic clove
1¼ cups chickpea flour
Oil for deep-frying

TO PREPARE

1. In a medium saucepan, over medium heat, add the milk, butter, salt and pepper. Use a microplane grater to grate the garlic clove over the pot, or just mince the garlic and throw it in. Heat until boiling.
2. Reduce the heat to low and slowly whisk in the chickpea flour. Whisk until the mixture is thick and smooth and begins to pull away from the side of the saucepan.
3. Spoon the batter out onto a greased rimmed baking sheet (a cookie sheet does nicely), making a layer half an inch thick. Use a spatula to smooth the top. Cool completely.
4. Cut the batter into 6 (3-inch) round circles. The top of a drinking glass dipped in chickpea flour works well for this purpose. Heat the oil to 350 degrees. Place paper towels on a baking sheet and set aside. Fry 2 fritters at a time for 3–4 minutes, turning over halfway through the frying until golden brown. Remove to paper towels to drain. Continue with remaining fritters. Makes 6 fritters.

SALAD AND ASSEMBLY

INGREDIENTS

¼ teaspoon toasted cumin seeds, ground
1½ teaspoons champagne vinegar
2 tablespoons olive oil
2 tablespoons grape-seed oil
¼ teaspoon salt
⅛ teaspoon pepper
1½ cups torn frisée
2 small cremini (ordinary white or brown) mushrooms, shaved or sliced thinly
1 tablespoon minced shallot

TO PREPARE

1. Make the dressing by whisking together the cumin, vinegar, olive and grape seed oils, salt and pepper in a bowl. (Olive oil can be substituted if you don't have any grape-seed oil, white or balsamic vinegar can be substituted for the champagne vinegar, and any kind of firm, non-dried mushroom (though not shiitake) can be substituted for cremini).

2. Combine the frisée, mushrooms, and shallot in a bowl. Add the dressing and gently toss.

3. Place a fritter on each plate. Place about 2 tablespoons of frisée salad on top and serve. With lots of napkins!

FALL SLAW WITH APPLES AND BACON

p. 17

CHICKEN LEGS WITH KUMQUATS, PRUNES AND GREEN OLIVES

p. 37

LANGER'S PASTRAMI SANDWICH

p. 67

JEFF DIETRICH'S BREAD PUDDING WITH WHISKEY SAUCE

p. 73

INA'S GRILLED GRUYÈRE, RED CABBAGE AND APPLE SANDWICH

p. 109

DEVILED EGGS

p. 116

ZANKOU CHICKEN

p. 117

William H. Johnson, *Come to Me, Little Children*

MANDARIN DELI SH)

Thy Will Be Done

ne Day At A Time

Paula Modersohn-Becker,
with Red Dress and

ST. EUGENE de MAZENOD
Patron of
Dysfunctional Families

SAN LUIS REY

Piet Mondrian, *Sun, Church in Zeeland*

Gala
& Exhibition
Grand Opening

Honoring **KEN BURNS**
Celebrating *CALIFORNIA CONTINUED*

H - 213.38
C - 213.29
hdkin
www.h

SLOW-ROASTED SHOULDER OF PORK

p. 127

**RED AND GOLDEN BEETS WITH BLOOD ORANGES,
ENDIVE, AND WALNUTS**

p. 135

QUINOA SALAD WITH GRILLED SCALLIONS, FAVAS, AND DATES

p. 147

ROSEMARY CORNCAKES

p. 157

≫ 14 ≪

Done with the Chart

Futile - the winds -
To a Heart in port -
Done with the Compass -
Done with the Chart!

Rowing in Eden -
Ah - the Sea!
Might I but moor - tonight -
In thee!

—Emily Dickinson

When I moved to LA—to start over, to expand my horizons—just finding my way around was a major challenge. It was 1990; broke, I bought a 1986 Thomas Guide at a yard sale and studied it like a textbook, memorizing the page numbers—Pasadena, 27; Santa Monica 49—as if they were math formulas.

Driving surface streets was nerve-wracking enough and, for months, all I could handle. The first time I drove the freeway was to the offices of the State Bar of California—downtown: 44, a page so clotted with activity it was almost completely black—for some sample exams. Getting there from my Palms apartment seemed roughly equivalent to crossing the Sahara, a daring, perhaps hours-long journey I was sure only LA's boldest drivers undertook. Plotting out my course that morning—the 10 east to the 110 north to the 4th Street exit—I envisioned trillions of cars, clouds of exhaust-fouled air, getting trapped in the wrong lane, missing my turn and ending up in Arizona.

Finally, I screwed up all my courage, got in my car, navigated the convoluted ganglia of streets around Robertson and then, miraculously, I was out on the freeway in a body of traffic propelling me inexorably forward to the distant, smog-shrouded towers of downtown. All the way there and back, I gripped the wheel, rigor-mortis rigid, the Thomas Guide—the reassuring grids, the 10 a friendly aorta pulsing off the page—open on the seat beside me. I had already had my bicycle stolen, gotten a street-cleaning ticket, and seen a jacaranda. But driving home that afternoon, sample exams in hand, I knew I was truly a resident of LA.

For a long time, I was too intent on finding my way to piece together my surroundings or much notice the local geography. I passed the bar, landed a job at 3731 Wilshire in Koreatown, drove down Venice Boulevard from Overland to Western Avenue every morning. One day, after a month or so, the smog lifted. I came home that afternoon and told Tim, "There are mountains back there! There's a giant range of *mountains* in back of downtown!"

He stared at me for a moment, his face suffused with pity. "Honey?" he said. "Why do you think they call it the *Valley?*"

I drove to court in Torrance, Norwalk, Van Nuys, drove so much and so often that driving my city became second nature. I drove to writing classes at UCLA, to dinner at a Schindler house in the Los Feliz Hills, to Mass in Boyle Heights. I drive all over the county to talk to other recovering drunks: a Watts board-and-care, the liver ward at Downey's Rancho Los Amigos, the prison in Chino.

After a couple of years, Tim and I moved east to Koreatown, with its grand old crumbling buildings, its teeming, noisy streets. Every weekend we went exploring and discovered whole new worlds. We followed Crenshaw all the way from its beginning at Wilshire to its ending in Palos Verdes, where it petered into a foot trail that we walked to the cliffs of the Pacific. We drove to Malibu and climbed Sandstone Peak, the stands of blue lupine taller than our heads, the air smelling of cedar and ripe peaches. We drove to Newport Beach for an Edward Hopper exhibit, to Claremont for a Mozart festival, to Artesia for tandoori and Gardena for udon and Westminster for pho, our tracks invisibly crisscrossed and backstitched across the pages of the Thomas Guide like the tracks of ants, tottering home the memories of art and music and shared meals like so many bits of masticated leaves.

After awhile, LA no longer felt unfamiliar and chaotic: it cohered into a kind of manic sense. Over time, somehow, imperceptibly, the city became not separate pages, but a living entity, of which I was one grateful, contributing cell.

Our horizons expanded so much that we eventually bought a Thomas Guide to the whole state. We drove to Santa Barbara, La Jolla, Joshua Tree. We drove up the coast, past San Luis Obispo and Big Sur and Santa Cruz, to Point Reyes, with its oyster and dairy farms, its miles of meandering coastline and historic inlets. It was beautiful, but the poetically named "marine layer" also made it—in July—frigid. We were camping and, after the third or fourth night of playing cribbage dressed in a double layer of polar fleece, Tim looked at me one morning and said, "I don't care if Sir Francis Drake did sail into here. At least LA is *warm*."

A few hours later, we were at a fruit stand on the 5 buying a cooler full of sodas and a five-dollar bag of cherries from a stringy guy in cowboy boots and a white ten-gallon hat. I took off my shoes, put on shorts, and drove barefoot for four hundred baking miles straight down the middle of the state, tossing cherry pits out the window, sipping sun-warmed Coke the temperature of tea.

On the treacherous upgrade of the Tejon Pass, cars sprawled on the turnouts, their hoods gaped open as if gasping for breath. Sweeping down between the mountains, the traffic got thicker, billboards loomed and a Carl's Jr. sign glowed, poisonously yellow, through a choking brown haze of smog. Merging with the teeming river of cars headed south from the Antelope Valley into town, I flashed for a minute on the majestic cliffs of Big Sur, the waves crashing on Stinson Beach, the peaceful, freezing cold mornings in Point Reyes.

Then a green sign reading "101—Hollywood" hove into view. Hollywood! The Vine Street exit, Rossmore to 6th to Wilton to 9th to Hobart—Salvadorean roach coaches, discarded sofas on the sidewalk, helicopters and gunfire—home! Tim and I turned to each other, crazed with happiness, and raised our fists in a silent cheer.

◊ ◊ ◊ ◊

Driving around my neighborhood—43, not that I've had to consult that page in ages—there's a Rite Aid going up in the empty lot on Crenshaw, a new Hollywood Video on the ground floor of the Wiltern Theatre. The Ralph's that was down on Olympic when we first moved here emigrated north to Western and 8th for a few months and is now a block east on Oxford. I pull in and, list in hand, troll the familiar aisles, thinking of the Crest coupons carefully toted from one location to another, the eggplants and whole wheat bread and tins of anchovies dutifully hauled home first from one store, then the next, the half-forgotten dinner parties with people whose numbers I've lost, the yellowing recipes cut from the Food section of the *Times*, the year the strawberries were so good, the season there were no avocados.

I still tend to think of my "past" as having taken place in New England but, putting the groceries in the car, it dawns on me that I've developed a history here, too. The 1986 Thomas Guide is still in the back seat, but it is not four years old anymore, it's thirteen; and it is no longer the '80 Celica I first bought, but an '89 Mazda; and I am not in my thirties anymore, but pushing fifty. When I look at the Thomas Guide now, I have to wear reading glasses.

That afternoon I am cleaning the bathroom mirror, Windex in one hand, paper towel in the other. Standing back to make sure I got the last stubborn toothpaste speck, mulling over whether we should spend our next vacation in Death Valley or Yosemite, I catch an unexpected glimpse of my face in repose. That is when I see the tracks radiating from the corners of my eyes, the little gullies around the lips, the freeway of faintly bulging vein in my left temple: the map of the face I keep hidden, even from myself.

It's like a head-on crash I never saw coming. When I embarked on a new life, when I set out nine years ago to transcend the past by learning to live in the present, I forgot to factor in this. Here in the land of golden dreams and eternal youth, I am growing old.

Stricken, my eyes descend to the counter, to the nasturtiums in their blown-glass vase, the afternoon sun falling on the flowers in such a way that some trick of refracted light makes it look as if the bright orange petals were veiled with violet. I stare at them for a long time: one person on one of thousands of blocks on one of 201 pages in the map of one city of 8 million in one of 50 states in one of hundreds of countries on one of 6 continents in one of 9 planets in an unimaginably huge, ever-expanding universe.

How odd, I think, how lovely! Purple, on nasturtiums! I never noticed that before.

COCONUT FLAN

I don't know where this recipe came from but I can tell you that it was hand-written on a half piece of lined, torn-out notebook paper and Xeroxed.

Shredded coconut in syrup is a delightful product I used to get at Liberio's Market (now closed) on 8th and Vermont Avenue, a half-mile from my K-town apartment. Coconut in heavy cane sugar syrup: who wouldn't like that? The can weighs about two pounds if you're lugging your provisions home on foot, as I usually was.

I love that whoever wrote the recipe didn't coddle. She (or he) assumed you know that sweetened condensed milk generally comes in a standard (14-ounce) size can, that you'd know what the command, "caramel-line mold" meant (I didn't, but figured it out), that you've cooked enough to be familiar with the idea of putting the pan you cook the thing in (here, called a mold) into a larger pan filled with water, and baking.

I made this once—along with shrimp in garlic, plantains, and black beans—when my little brother Joe's punk band, the Queers, were in town. Hughbie (O'Neill), the drummer, was still alive then. He died a few years later of brain cancer, and every time I make coconut flan I think of him and how you never, ever regret cooking a meal for people, but you may very well regret *not* having cooked for them.

There is absolutely nothing that is "good" for you here—well, maybe the eggs—and it's to die for. Settle back with a generous helping. Regard that glistening layer of caramel-colored sugar, larded with candied coconut. Put on a Queers song: "Noodlebrain," maybe, or "Next Stop, Rehab." And have a second helping.

INGREDIENTS

1 can sweetened condensed milk
4 eggs
1 large (18 ounces) can shredded coconut in syrup
1 cup sugar

TO PREPARE

1. Caramel-line mold with sugar (i.e. melt sugar over medium heat until it's caramel colored, and then pour it over the bottom and sides of a glass dish. I've used loaf pans, square pans, and a small rectangular pan—they all work fine. But you want to use glass).

2. Beat eggs lightly. Add condensed milk. Fill milk can with coconut syrup (you'll have some left) and add to eggs and milk. Mix well. Pour into mold. Place mold in center of large pan containing warm water to cover bottom of mold. Bake at 350 degrees for about 1½ hours. Cool in the refrigerator. Serve cold.

⇒ 15 ⇐

Rivers and Tides

The first really beautiful and useful movie I've seen this year (2003) is called *Rivers and Tides: Andy Goldsworthy Working with Time*. The subject is an artist who makes "sculptures" out of, among other things, leaves, rocks, sand, sticks, roots, and skeins of sheep's wool, many of which fall in upon themselves, or melt, or are borne away on the incoming tide.

In the opening scene it's four a.m., somewhere on the coast of Nova Scotia, and Goldsworthy is hard at work. He bites off pieces of icicle; shapes them with the heat from his lips and tongue and hands; and connects them, barely breathing, until he's formed a spiral—a spiral of ice!—to glorify the rays of the rising sun that will melt it. And in turn the sun glorifies the sculpture, brings it alive, completes the process of creation—"I didn't realize it would shine through on both sides!" exclaims Goldsworthy, who is willing to let the vagaries of wind, rain, and air both bring his works to fruition and destroy them. Watching a cairn he's painstakingly constructed on a beach gradually submerge itself beneath the encroaching waves, he seems on the verge of tears—not because his work is going to go for "nothing," but from a sense of awe. "The work has been given to the sea as a gift, and the sea has taken the gift and made more of it than I could have ever hoped or dreamed," he says, as the topmost stone disappears beneath the ocean. "And there's something to think about there when it comes to the shocks and upheavals of our own lives."

Goldsworthy lives in Penpont, Scotland, and, as the camera pans to expanses of green grass and cobblestoned streets and the spire of a weathered old church, he notes that you have to live in a place a long time, longer than four or five years, to get the feel of it. "You have to see the children waiting at the bus stop grow up and have their own children," he explains. *Yes indeed,* I think, harking back from my seat at West LA's Nuart Theatre to my own K-town street: *Why just the other day on the sidewalk I saw that cute little second-grader who used to help me with the groceries, except he's all grown up now, with the tent-like pants and shaved head of a gangbanger, and he was making out with a teenaged girl who looked like she was about to give birth any minute.*

"You have to see people being born and people dying," Goldsworthy continues, and I think of another neighbor, Oscar, and the day five years ago the ambulance came and took his lover Michael, who had AIDS, through the courtyard in a gurney, and about how when Michael was at Queen of Angels I called him and in his delirium he said, "Thank God at least we have our health!" and how two days later he died. I think about the morning four years ago when my mother called from New Hampshire to say that my father wasn't going to make it; and the afternoon three years ago when the doctor from Good Sam called to tell me the biopsy had come back malignant, and the day last week when I went out to the graffitied alley, got in my car, and drove down to the Central Courthouse to file the proof of service showing I'd served Tim by certified mail, because he lives back east again now, with divorce papers.

I think about how for long stretches life can seem to be nothing *but* shocks and upheavals. I think about how the whole eleven years I've lived in my beautiful apartment I've complained about the noise—the Korean kids next door, the produce trucks blaring "Turkey in the Straw"—and how I looked out the window to the courtyard one afternoon last week, and the scales fell from my eyes, and I saw the pink camellias and the gold hibiscus and the ficus trees with their leaves the yellow-green of new lettuce, and realized for the first time in months: *I live in paradise.* I think about how, like the sun shattering through a spiral of ice that will melt—and in time emerge in some other form—we are broken apart and put together again whether we want to be or not, with or without our cooperation, whether we live in a secluded Nova Scotia bay or the middle of Los Angeles.

And ever since, for a couple of weeks now, I've been thinking of the last frame of *Rivers and Tides,* when Goldsworthy flings a handful of loose snow into the air and, sculpted by the wind, it gathers itself for one aching second into a shape you can hardly see—then is gone.

ROMESCO SAUCE

Adapted from *Sunday Suppers at Lucques*, by Suzanne Goin

In K-town, almost every block has its own produce truck. What with our glut of Wal-Mart, Costco and Food 4 Less stores, the white, panel van produce truck, in fact, may be the last bastion of the mom-and-pop store. Ours had "Flores," a crude painting of a cornucopia, and the address—935 South Hobart—stenciled on the side, as if it were a permanent storefront, which in a way, it was.

In the front of the truck would be Alberto, with three or four kids wound around the stick shift. In back, the interior was cool and dim, with shelves on either side and an old pair of hanging scales. In the morning, a little plastic case held pastries; in the afternoon, a battered Igloo cooler contained cans of soda floating in the melting ice. There were always bunches of browning plantains, piles of limes, a hairy coconut or two. There was everything you needed to make a chili or huevos rancheros.

I loved the down-home feel of being able to wander out in my slippers, while the water boiled for tea, for a single egg, or an onion, or a mango, or laundry change.

Romesco is a thick, richly textured purée of tomatoes, nuts, and chiles that comes by way of Catalonia and can be served with crackers or raw vegetables, presented alongside seafood, chicken, or eggs, or simply eaten plain with a spoon, closed eyes, and a sigh.

You wouldn't find a hazelnut on the produce truck in a million years. But you for sure could find an ordinary tomato and either dried or fresh ancho chiles.

Romesco can't be described, only experienced: a revelation. It's loaded with oil (which is one reason I, personally, like it), so a bit goes a long way.

INGREDIENTS

10 ancho chiles, soaked in warm water for an hour, then dried and seeded
Salt
¼ cup almonds, toasted
¼ cup hazelnuts, toasted
1 clove garlic, chopped
1 inch-thick slice of country bread, fried in olive oil until golden brown,
then cut into ½-inch cubes

1 whole tomato, halved, roasted at 375 degrees for 30 minutes
1 tablespoon chopped flat-leaf parsley
1¼ cups extra-virgin olive oil
½ lemon, for juicing

TO PREPARE

1. Toast nuts in 375 degree oven for 8–10 minutes (keep an eye on them so they don't burn).
2. In a heavy sauté pan, heat 2 tablespoons of oil and sauté the chiles for five minutes. (I often use dried, in which case I soften them first for half an hour in boiling water). Season with salt and set aside.
3. In a food processor, blend the nuts, garlic, and bread cubes by pulsing until ground together.
4. Add chiles and pulse for another minute.
5. Add roasted tomatoes and parsley.
6. With the food processor running on low, slowly pour in olive oil until you have a purée. (You will think you're adding too much oil, but you aren't).
7. Season to taste with salt and lemon.

⇒ 16 ⇐

Food for the Middle of the Night

In *The Force of Character*, depth psychologist James Hillman's book on aging, he observes:

> So much goes on at night; not only dreams and reminiscences and prayers; not only fears, those visiting demons who sit on the edge of your bed and recount your blunders and worries, and then fly off (as vampires do) as morning finally comes. Even more insistent are pressing toilet calls.

I myself have a whole other life at night: sweating, tossing, turning, agonizing. Night is when I review undone tasks. Night is when I imagine dying. Night is when I look around my bedroom and think: *I'm 55—why buy a curtain rod now?* Night is when I pray. I pray for my sister Jeanne, my mother, my whole family, my late father, my friend Maureen, who died of mouth cancer, my friend Michael, who died of cirrhosis, the people in prison, the people on death row, the people in war zones, especially children, all abused children, all children, the people who are being tortured, all the suffering and sick, the bewildered, the pissed off, the people who've been sexually molested, the people who've molested them, all addicts and alcoholics, everywhere. All the people who have asked me to pray for them: priests, women in abusive relationships, mothers of addicts, husbands who are taking care of wives with Alzheimer's, people who can't stop drinking, people who hate themselves, people in the grip of OCD, people who are sad, people who are in despair, people who are broke. And again, always and forever, people who are lonely.

I pray and sometimes, I eat. To me, the ultimate comfort food is a grilled cheese sandwich, and the ultimate grilled cheese sandwich looks like this: Velveeta cheese, cheap white bread, real butter, cooked on the No. 7 black cast-iron frying pan, the smallest of the nested set, by my little sister Meredith in the kitchen at 108 Post Road in North Hampton, New Hampshire. Golden crispy, cheese oozing, cut on the diagonal, served on a green melamine plate, with a folded over cheap white embossed paper napkin. Logs snapping in the fireplace. Preferably snowing. Muffled sound of the plow going by. Eaten propped up on the couch in the living room, the one by Dad's chair, with the reading lamp. A book at my elbow—*The Wind in the Willows*, maybe, or *The Yearling*. On the TV, *The Waltons* or *The Twilight Zone*.

Those days are gone, but I still love a grilled cheese, usually with Trader Joe's Dubliner cheese, oatmeal bread, and, always, real butter (a few thinly sliced tomatoes, or halved cherry tomatoes don't hurt either).

A cup of hot chocolate is the essential accompaniment.

In the olden days, this would have been made with Hershey's powdered chocolate; milk from Runnymede Farm on Atlantic Avenue, poured from a glass bottle delivered by Mr. Gilman; and pure cane sugar. These days I free-pour a cup or so of milk into a saucepan (almond milk, with a drop of almond extract, also works), dump in a heaping soupspoon and a half of cocoa powder (Hershey's still, if for no other reason than they haven't changed the container in decades), turn the heat on high, turn down to medium after a couple of minutes, throw in sugar to taste, whisk when the mixture starts to warm, and make sure I don't then get too engrossed in rearranging the cupboards or scrubbing the counter to notice the chocolate is boiling and about to spill over.

The cup is also important. I have a little collection of coffee cups, many of them chipped and stained, that are like members of my family. There's the elegant French cup with thin straight sides and a green glaze somewhere between grass and lime that I bought at the late and lamented Dona Flor's on Newbury Street in Boston. There's the Talavera, snow white, turquoise, deep blue, and yolk-yellow, that Tim bought for me years ago at a shop in Old Town Pasadena (also closed). There's the Japanese cup, a glazed putty color with iridescent royal blue blotches given to me by my friend Judy when she was cleaning out her studio that at first glance didn't grab me but from which I am now inseparable.

And the sugar? That's spooned from Nana's blue-and-white sugar bowl, part of the twelve-piece place setting set of china she borught over on the boat from Ireland, and that I inherited when she died. That sugar bowl speaks to me of all that is safe, that is secure, that is of the ocean, that is love.

INA'S GRILLED GRUYÈRE, RED CABBAGE, AND APPLE SANDWICH

If you want a Reuben, go to Langer's. If you want a rich, slightly sloppy sandwich, redolent of the fall harvest but without the heavy meat, try this. A whisper of red onion, the sit-up-straight rigor of caraway and rye, the sharpness of red wine vinegar are balanced by the sweetness of apple, the consolation of butter, and the softness of melted gruyère cheese.

Personally, I'm for any recipe in which the word "griddle" appears.

INGREDIENTS

3 tablespoons butter, divided, plus more for griddle
1 red onion, thinly sliced
½ small head red cabbage, about ¾ pound, quartered, cored, thinly sliced
2 tablespoons red wine vinegar
2 tablespoons plus 1½ teaspoons sugar, divided
½ teaspoon caraway seeds
¼ teaspoon salt
Freshly ground pepper
1 large Granny Smith apple, peeled, halved, cored, thinly sliced
Dijon mustard, to taste
8 slices each hearty rye bread
2½ ounces gruyère cheese slices

TO PREPARE

1. Heat 2 tablespoons of butter in a 10-inch nonstick skillet over medium-high heat. When the butter is sizzling, add the onion and cook, stirring often, until softened but not brown, about 4 minutes. Add the cabbage and vinegar. Cook gently, covered, until the cabbage is tender but still

textured, about 12 minutes. Add 2 tablespoons of sugar, the caraway seeds, salt and pepper to taste. Cook gently 5 minutes longer, stirring often to prevent burning.

2. Toss the apple slices with the remaining 1½ teaspoons of sugar in a large bowl. Heat 1 tablespoon of butter in an 8-inch nonstick skillet over medium-high heat. When the butter starts to brown, add the apple. Cook until golden and tender but still intact, about 6–8 minutes, stirring often.

3. To assemble, generously spread dijon mustard on 4 bread slices. Cover the mustard with the warm apple. Cover the apples with a cheese slice. Divide the warm cabbage equally among the remaining 4 slices of bread. Place a cheese slice on the cabbage. Leave the sandwiches open-faced for cooking; then close after cooking.

4. Heat the oven to 250 degrees.

5. Heat the griddle over medium heat and lightly butter. Place 2 open-faced sandwiches on the griddle. Cook, tented with foil, until the cheese is melted, about 4 minutes. Close the sandwich, pressing it lightly together. Turn it over and place on a baking sheet. Keep warm in the oven while cooking the remaining sandwiches. Serve warm.

⇒ 17 ⇐

Appalachian Summer

I'm the type who, given a choice between a brand-new apartment with a dishwasher, wall-to-wall carpet, and a Mexican gardener; and a falling-down place with old slanting wood floors, gaps in the french windows, and a crumbling balcony where you can have your own plants to kill, will choose the old place every time.

Thus to me, my way-below-market-value K-town apartment was a gem. I had a courtyard, French windows, hand-painted tile in the bathroom and kitchen, and a balcony filled with succulents and bromeliads and cacti I'd grown from cuttings filched from friends' gardens and median strips. I had Oriental and kilim rugs, paintings, icons, sconces, crucifixes, incense. I had a living room with crown moldings, a fireplace mantel carved with cherubs and bunches of grapes, and walls painted a contemplative deep gray-green called Sparrow. People walked in and said, It's so you! They said, It's so warm! They said, You'll never find another place like this.

Something about that last began to irk me. Perhaps I never would, but perhaps eighteen years in any apartment—especially one that was more or less in the ghetto—was also long enough. I'd come in some sense to believe that my identity lay in that apartment. The apartment, with its combined weight of decades of mementoes, photos, keepsakes, and journals, had become a kind of psychic albatross. Did I really need the falling-apart Fitzgerald Reader—a "gift" (exchange, really)—from the guy who'd deflowered me? Did I need the scratched-beyond-repair LP of Dylan's

Blonde on Blonde I'd listened to as a junior in high school—especially when I no longer owned a turntable? Did I need to be sleeping in the same bedroom in which I'd slept for ten years with my ex-husband?

No. I hadn't needed any of that that for a long time. I'd reached the same kind of critical fear-versus-faith mass I'd reached fifteen years earlier when I'd quit my job as a lawyer. If I had to live beneath a freeway underpass, I'd figured then, so be it: I had to write. And now, if I had to live in a broom closet, so be it: I had to let go of this apartment.

Another person, perhaps, would have simply looked for another apartment. But that would have been too easy, too straightforward. In fact, the move from my apartment was the culmination of an unexplained urge I'd felt for some time: namely, to take off and spend several months in silence and solitude. Clearly, I'd been called to writing—but was that enough? Did I have some further, other, vocation? Was I called to a deeper surrender—the what, how, and why of which I couldn't yet imagine?

Maybe I would start a new life! Maybe I would let go of the whole city of Los Angeles! So I cobbled together three months at a writer's residency in Taos, a forty-day silent retreat further east, a week with old friends in Nashville, and a month or two or three (it turned out to be one) at the Franciscan Appalachian Hermitage in West Virginia. And then I gave notice on my Koreatown apartment, sold or gave away most of my belongings, packed up my white '96 Celica convertible, and took off on what I billed as an open-ended sabbatical.

I had my three months in Taos. I had my forty-day retreat, billed as a "Desert Experience," a description I learned was a gross understatement. I'd worked myself into a "thin place," as the Irish say: somewhere between heaven and earth, in liminal space and time. I was a bit homesick, a bit bereft. Had I made a mistake to leave LA? Why was I feeling I had so few people to talk to? Why, as I prepared to launch into the next leg of my journey, was I feeling so unmoored?

I've been a bluegrass fan since my youth. Crazed for company and approaching West Virginia, I pictured informal bands on every street corner—settin' on bales of hay, tuning their fiddles, just waiting for *me* to show up so they could launch into a killer rendition of "Body and Soul" or "Highway of Sorrow." I pictured striking up conversations with such folks. I pictured making friends.

One day soon after landing in Spencer, a town of seven thousand in the northwest part of the state, I read in the local paper of a covered-dish potluck at the nearby Otto Community Center. That Friday night, I made a batch of deviled eggs, mentally reprised some of my best stories, and set out.

Otto turned out to be about twenty-five winding—actually, that's redundant; every road in West Virginia is winding—miles outside of town. The hollers were blanketed in wildflowers and overhung with tall, old-growth trees. I arrived at the potluck to find an intriguing casserole of sliced hot dogs and cream of mushroom soup cloaked with a thick layer of cornbread. An equally interesting dessert combined graham crackers, Cool Whip, strawberry Jell-O, sour cream, strawberry pie filling and canned walnuts. And the twenty or thirty people in attendance managed to be simultaneously totally accommodating and totally, *totally* uninterested in me and my "story." I liked them tremendously for this. At first, I was afraid maybe my black jeans (and black muscle shirt, Pumas, and belt) had marked me out as Wiccan. But then I realized I'd made the exact same mistake people make when they watch TV and form the stereotypical opinion that every Los Angeleno spends his or her life being randomly killed by landslides, earthquakes, freeway pileups, snipers, and rioting minorities. These folks didn't need another friend. They *had* friends. They had families, by whom they were surrounded. They weren't remotely fired up to have an existentially tormented, spiritually conflicted, temporarily homeless West Coaster in their midst.

Happily, some other Spencer folks were, and as is so often the case, they were the clean and sober drunks, junkies, potheads, crackheads, and meth freaks in town. One such character introduced himself to me a few days later on the steps of a local church as Dane. "Dane?" I asked. "No, Dane." "You mean Dane? D-A-N-E?" "No, DANE." "Oh, *Dean!*" the light finally dawned.

Dean held forth on the deleterious effects of home-brewed corn liquor on the human esophagus, and Ernest allowed that someone had once snitched on his moonshining friends back in Tennessee and they'd drawn lots to see who'd shoot the guy.

I took in the Ripley 4th of July parade (pronounced PAY-rade). I ate "biscuits," a local delicacy which consisted of two thick globs of doughy bread, with about ten slices of bacon in the middle. I attended the Mountain State Art and Crafts Fair, watched an iron forger for a spell, and bought a very cool eleven-dollar key chain made from a spiraled-out piece of twisted metal which I promptly took off, threaded through a piece of leather cord, and made into a necklace.

But mostly I hung out with LaDean and Annie. I loved these gals. They toted around their own personal giant thermoses of coffee, they smoked like fiends (LaDean rolled her own, from tobacco bought in bulk from the smoke and beer shop), and their purses were stocked with fistfuls of Hershey's Kisses and Smarties. One night, we decided to take a field trip to the nearby city of Parkersburg. Annie drove, LaDean rode shotgun, and I sat in the back so as to be able to open both windows and thereby avoid asphyxiation. LaDean immediately pulled out a purple plastic lighter, torched up, and passed around a Tupperware container of candy. Annie took a meditative drag on her Marlboro Light 100 and mused, "We could go Route 14, but that damn road's crookeder 'n a dog's hind leg."

With Annie as tour guide, once in Parkersburg we stopped in at Fort Boreman, a Civil War site overlooking a stunning view of the Little Kanawha and Ohio Rivers, a couple of charming bridges, and Blennerhassett Island. We toured the city's historical section with its Victorian and Queen Anne mansions. We wondered if Starbucks was open—Spencer had no decent coffeehouse of any kind—but it was past nine and everything was closed.

I'd planned on staying in Appalachia a couple of months, maybe even three. But I'd been on the road, specifically in small, somewhat remote towns, for five months. I could totally get behind shopping at Dollar General and Wal-Mart. I didn't mind driving to the Spencer library every day to check my email. Living in a cabin with the shower in the bedroom, a small snake problem, and the only shelf space for my makeup above the kitchen sink didn't faze me.

What did faze me was that I began to feel that if I stayed much longer, I wouldn't be "on pilgrimage" anymore; I'd be hiding out. I'd gone on the road partly as a money-saving measure, and partly because I'd felt called to an extended period of solitude and silence. But I'd had my silence, and I began to realize it was time to take what I'd learned or absorbed or pratfallen over and return to the world. In one way I hated leaving "so soon," and in another, I was itching to head home.

Our goodbye get-together convened at the Spencer McDonald's. Annie and Linda, a big-hearted, big-voiced Texas gal, drove the twenty-five miles from Ripley. I picked up LaDean. The four of us sat in a corner booth, drinking coffees and Diet Cokes, and I'm still not sure how it happened, but somehow we ended up taking fifteen or twenty minutes apiece and telling— we'd already shared bits and pieces of our stories—what it was like when we drank, and how we got sober. I don't want to violate anyone's privacy, but I think I can safely say there were enough booze-related accidents and injuries, enough across-state-lines statutory rapes, marriages, and divorces, enough broken limbs, broken promises, and broken hearts that we all felt right at home. There were also enough hard-won family truces, reparations made, and tiny glints of hope to give me, for one, reason to persevere another day. LaDean presented each of us with a small talismanic rock she'd hand-painted with various shades of nail polish, sanded down, and glazed. The three of them gave me a beautiful card signed with love and good wishes.

Afterwards, we went outside and sat on the curb in the shade so the gals could smoke a last cigarette. Part of the sadness of travel is the sense of the alternate lives we could have lived, the day-to-day relationships we could have formed, the community in which we could have participated and that, because we live in real time and real space and are going to die at the end, we are never, this side, going to be able to. But along with the sadness goes the sense that the people whom we do meet this side are fellow travelers; that in some other realm we have been ordained to know and to be sustained, however fleetingly, by each other's faces and voices and light.

Finally, there was nothing left to do but nose little pebbles and squashed-out cigarette butts around on the McDonald's parking lot asphalt with the toes of our shoes.

"I wish you could stay."

"Me, too."

"We loved having you here."

"I loved being here."

"God sent you to us," Annie said.

I looked out over the smoked-blue hills of West Virginia. Maybe. But to this day, I think God sent them to me.

DEVILED EGGS

Deviled eggs are *the* great all-occasion potluck item. Nothing could be easier or more foolproof than whipping up a batch.

INGREDIENTS

Eggs (however many you want to use)
Mayonnaise to taste
Mustard to taste
Paprika to taste

TO PREPARE

1. Take however many eggs you want to use, put them in a pot of enough cold water to cover, bring to a boil, let boil for a minute or so, take off the heat, cover and let sit for ten or twelve minutes. Then drain, run cold water over them, and peel immediately.

2. Let the eggs cool completely while you sweep the floor, listen to the birds, or rearrange your spice cabinet. Cut eggs in half lengthwise (the long way) and scoop out the yolks with a spoon into a bowl. Mix in mayonnaise to taste, at least a couple of tablespoons per six eggs, and start with half a teaspoon or so of powdered mustard. I don't know why, but only powdered mustard will do. The Colman's yellow tin can, which is almost the same color as the yolks, is best for maximum nostalgia effect. Mix that all up with a fork and pile back into the hollowed-out hard-boiled egg white halves.

3. Then—this, too, is essential: sprinkle lightly with paprika. The paprika, too, and for the same reason as the mustard, should come out of a can. We probably used some generic brand like Finast or Ann Page when I was a kid. These days Pride of Szeged Hungarian style Paprika, in its red-and-white can, fills in nicely.

⤜ 18 ⤛

The Traveler Returns: Zankou Chicken

I can pretty much pinpoint the moment I knew I was going to return to LA from my "sabbatical." It wasn't the moment I thought: *I miss the light in Southern California.* It wasn't the moment I thought: *LA is where I can be most creative, or grow the most, or most fully serve my fellow man.* It was the moment my friend Maud emailed me and said, "Heather, you won't believe it. They're selling little containers of the garlic sauce from Zankou Chicken at Jons."

You haven't really lived till you've been to Zankou Chicken. I'm talking the original location of course, in a grungy strip mall on the northeast corner of Sunset and Normandie. The one with the parking lot full of surly Armenian cab drivers and triple-parked cars. The one so redolent of the luscious smells of roast chicken and juicy glistening shawerma that you'd almost pay just to stand in line. The one where the garlic sauce—a seemingly mild but über-potent white paste, the exact composition of which remains a fiercely guarded secret and which no living man, woman, or child outside the Iskenderian family has yet been able to parse—all began.

But it's never really about the food, or only about the food. It's about the layers of meaning and memory above, below, and running through the food. When I go to Zankou I don't just go for the chicken or the garlic sauce. I go thinking of the dark underbelly of the immigrant dream. I go knowing that in 2003, spurred by family rivalries/resentments and the fact that he was dying of cancer, the scion of the Zankou franchise came home one night, pulled out a 9mm semiautomatic Browning, and shot to death his mother, sister, and himself. I go thinking of California journalist Mark Arax, whose own father had been gunned down in a Fresno barroom decades before, who wangled his way into the bosom of the Iskenderian family, and wrote an essay called "Legend of Zankou" (which you can read in his *West of the West*).

I go thinking of Jonathan Gold, Pulitzer Prize-winning food writer and true LA treasure who, via some long-ago column, turned me on to Zankou in the first place. Though we've never actually spoken, I feel I have a history with Jonathan Gold. He introduced me to Vim's on 8th and Vermont (greasy-spoon Thai), Dow Shaw (which morphed into Heavy Noodling, which morphed into JTYH, now in Rosemead) (insanely delicious shanxi knife-cut noodles), and the Hong Kong Deli (pork chop rice, fish puff soup) for dim sum. He wrote a piece after the 1992 riots that moved me to tears. I once attended an ALOUD event at the downtown library in which he took part. Afterwards I approached the stage trembling, clasped my hands before my heart, like St. Thérèse of Lisieux appealing to Pope Leo XIII to please, *please* allow her to enter the cloister at Carmel at the age of fifteen, and croaked, simply: "Thank you." Gold responded with as much grace as any human being under the circumstances could have been expected to. He replied, "Heh-hey, okay then," and backed very, very slowly away.

Famously, for a while when he was in his early twenties, Gold "had only one clearly articulated ambition: to eat at least once at every restaurant on Pico Boulevard." Pico is not, at first glance, one of LA's most promising thoroughfares, but that he managed to mine its riches and discover a universe in the process was exactly the point. "Pico, in a certain sense," he observed of the experience, "was where I learned to eat. I also saw my first punk-rock show on Pico, was shot at, fell in love, bowled a 164, witnessed a knife fight, took cello lessons, raised chickens, ate Oki Dogs and heard X, Ice Cube, Hole, and Willie Dixon perform (though not together) on Pico."

From 2,500 miles away, the image of that little container of garlic sauce reminded me that in Los Angeles, I had walked my own unpromising streets, pondered my own questions, developed my own passion for plumbing its mysteries. I'd gone away in part to write, but that single superb sentence of Gold's reminded me that if it's never only about the food, it's also never only about the writing. It's about streets, neighborhoods, heart. I needed to come home.

So I came home, and I haven't stopped writing since.

Which brings me back to Zankou. Go. Have yourself a Styrofoam container of juicy chicken or shawerma or falafel. Rejoice that the Iskenderian family is back on its feet and opening Zankou outlets all over Southern Cal. Groove on the pickled vegetables: saffron yellow, turmeric orange, sumac purple. Get juice on your chin. Wipe your greasy hands on the bottom of your shirt. Eat deeply of the garlic sauce. Descend into the garlic sauce. Maybe, though it hasn't to anyone else, it will yield its secret to you.

ZANKOU CHICKEN

TO PREPARE

1. Take a break from cooking.
2. Seriously, get some takeout.

⮞ 19 ⮜

Goodbye to All That

Shortly after returning from my trip in the fall of 2010, I started a blog. This was one of my first entries.

> "Men travel faster now, but I do not know if they go to better things."
>
> —Willa Cather

I had many adventures on my sabbatical. I learned many things, most of them completely different than the ones I expected to learn. I'd expected the internal movement to be toward a further paring down, more asceticism. But the trip broke something, perhaps many things, open in me that I didn't even know were dammed up. I saw how carefully I control my life so that certain things are kept in and certain things are kept out. I saw how often I mask fear with self-righteousness. I saw that I experience the smallest failure, disappointment, or "rejection" as devastating, and that I had developed a whole way of being that revolved around avoiding those things. I saw how attached I was to the idea of myself as a solitary, a "hermit." I also, for perhaps the first time in my life, experienced the old saw, "You take yourself with you wherever you go," as a good thing. I was glad to have myself along. I can't think of better company. And perhaps because of that, since I returned I've also been more open to other people; new possibilities.

I've been cat-sitting for the last five weeks in an apartment in West Hollywood. I've enjoyed my time here. Every Monday I get to walk across the street to the Plummer Park farmers market. I get to walk to Trader Joe's, Ralphs, Jons, Target, and the Will and Ariel Durant branch of the public library. Runyon Canyon is a little overrun for my taste, but I've discovered the residential streets to the west that run past the Wattles Farm Community Garden, a jungle of roses, towering calla lilies, and prickly pear cacti. I've discovered that if you go far enough north, and are willing to walk up a steep enough hill, you come to the end of Curson Avenue, a street most of us know better several miles south, around Wilshire, as the one where you start looking for parking if you're going to visit the LA County Museum of Art.

I have always been drawn to borders: the juxtaposition of civilization and wilderness, the conscious and the subconscious, here and eternity. I love that if you follow any street in LA far enough it will eventually peter out into either the mountains or the ocean. Crenshaw ends at the Pacific in Palos Verdes. I once had a tax accountant in West Hills (RIP Jack Willow); a trip to his office involved driving east on Roscoe Boulevard, a main San Fernando Valley drag, to the place where it ends in a stand of fennel.

Next Wednesday, I'll be moving into a big, beautiful house in Silver Lake. I'm going to have a roommate, a possibility I would never in my wildest dreams have considered five years, or one year, or even nine months ago. I have no idea how this will pan out. All I know is that last night, toward dusk, I walked to the top of Curson. I paused to catch my breath, then turned and, looking south, stood for a minute on the foot-wide lip of concrete that marks the end of someone's driveway and the beginning of wilderness.

The city, resplendent, was gilded in a smog-tinged pink haze. I thought of all the places I've been and all the places I still have to go. I tried to make out the 900 South block of Hobart Boulevard in Koreatown—my home for so long—but, already, I was too far away.

PHO GA: VIETNAMESE CHICKEN NOODLE SOUP

Pho (pronounced feuh, sort of) is a whole culture here in LA: we have pho experts, pho purists, pho bloggers, arcane cookers of arcane types of pho. I make no claim to any of that. You can get a better bowl of pho on any street corner here, and for cheaper, than you could possibly make at home. But getting to buy a little plastic bag of star anise and a cheap paper box of rock sugar is a treat not to be taken lightly.

Those, along with delicious tia to (heart-haped leaves, purple on one side, deep green on the other), anise basil, bean sprouts, big red net bags of ginger, and all the other ingredients for my recipe could be found at the A-Grocery Warehouse at 1487 W. Sunset, a mile or so away from my new home.

This recipe suggests, for a smoky, sweet flavor, setting a big halved onion, papery husk and all, and a chunk of unpeeled ginger under the broiler to char. Again, a small and thrilling adventure.

INGREDIENTS

1 4–5 pound whole chicken
1 whole onion, unpeeled and cut in half
3-inch chunk of ginger, unpeeled

(A) BROTH SPICES

2 tablespoons whole coriander seeds
4 whole cloves
2 whole star anise
2 tablespoons sugar (or rock sugar)
2 tablespoons fish sauce
Small bunch of cilantro stems only, tied in bunch with twine

(B) ACCOMPANIMENTS AT TABLE

1 pound dried rice noodles (about ¼-inch wide)
2 cups bean sprouts, washed
Cilantro tops—leaves and tender stems
½ cup shaved red onions
½ lime, cut into 4 wedges
Sriracha hot sauce
Hoisin sauce
Sliced chile

TO PREPARE

1. Place ginger and onion on a small baking sheet. The top of the onion should be about 4 inches from the oven's heating element. Set to broil on high for 15 minutes. Turn the onion and ginger occasionally, to get an even char. The skin should get dark and the onion/ginger should get soft. After cooling, rub to get the charred skin off the onion and use a butter knife to scrape the skin off the ginger. Slice ginger into thick slices. In a large stockpot, fill with water and boil. With a sharp cleaver, carve the chicken breast meat off and reserve. With the rest of chicken whacking hard through the bones to get sections about 3 inches big. The more bone that is exposed, the more marrow that gets in the broth (translation: rich, flavorful). You can even whack several places along the bone just to expose more marrow. When the water boils, add chicken sections (not breast) and boil on high for 5 minutes. You'll see lots of foam come up to the surface. Drain, rinse your chicken of the scum and wash your pot thoroughly. Refill with about 4 quarts of clean, cold water.

2. Add chicken, chicken breast meat, onion, ginger and all of (A) in the pot and cover. Turn heat to high—let it come to a boil, then immediately turn heat to low. Prop lid up so that steam can escape. After 15 minutes, remove the chicken breasts, shred with your fingers when cooled, and set aside (you'll serve shredded chicken breast with the finished soup). With a large spoon, skim the surface of any impurities in the broth. Skimming every 20 minutes ensures a clear broth. Simmer a total of 1–1½ hours. Taste and adjust seasoning with more fish sauce and or sugar.

3. Strain the broth, discard solids. Prepare noodles as per directions on package. Ladle broth, add shredded chicken breast and soft noodles into your favorite Talavera bowls. Have (B) ingredients set at table for each person to add to his or her bowl: cut-up limes, shallot, scallions, cilantro, tia to, anise basil, hoisin, and fish sauce.

4. Pour tall glasses of stevia-sweetened ginger tea.

☙ 20 ❧

Pilgrim Feet

My approach to life is pretty simple: take a walk, wherever you are; observe whatever's around you. By "walk," I don't mean the fetishistic activity that involves leg weights, a water bottle carrier, a backpack, an odometer, a satellite system, and an ipod. I'm talking grabbing your keys, keeping your eyes peeled, and taking an hour, two-hour stroll for the sheer, exuberant wonder of the enterprise.

I check out the flowers and the birds. I smile, or at least meet people's eyes and acknowledge them as human beings. At least once in awhile people will smile back. People's faces are transfigured when they smile.

Sometimes I picture leaving invisible bits of my body and blood behind, little energy trails of calorie-burnt-up heat, on the LA streets where I walk. I walk for all the people who can't walk: the people in wheelchairs, the old, the sick, the people in solitary confinement, the people in straitjackets, the babies.

I've walked all over my neighborhood, and every neighborhood I've ever lived in. But mostly I walk down Sunset Boulevard, around Edgecliffe, Lucile and Micheltorena, both north and south of Sunset. All the better if my aging body aches a little; if I'm a little cold, a little tired, a little lonely, a little depressed. I study the shadows on the sidewalk, the trunks of trees, the clouds. Sometimes when I'm hurrying along Sunset Boulevard, I think of some lines from a Psalm: *He makes my feet swift as those of hinds/He enables me to go upon the heights.*

To walk to Mass makes for an especially beautiful exchange, a kind of full circle. I'll walk through the hot streets of Atwater, then go to Holy Trinity and sit awhile before the Blessed Sacrament. Or I'll wander around downtown, then go to noon Mass at the cathedral. I need to regularly break bread with people I haven't handpicked. I need to ritualize letting go in order to participate in something greater than myself.

Surely paradise must be very much like Southern California in September. Sometimes I wish the long afternoons of early fall would last forever. Recently, I was headed to a seven o'clock Taize "hour of prayer" at St. Francis of Assisi in Silver Lake, but first I took a long walk, up and around the steep streets north of Sunset Boulevard, lost in thought, the air rich with the fragrance of lavender and wild fennel and sage. Way up near the top of the hill, I ran into a shirtless man who was also walking.

Apparently we'd passed one another because he stopped and said "Is this your regular walk? I saw you up at the crest."

"Yeah, I'm out here all the time, wandering about."

"I live over by the Franklin Hills but I thought I'd come over this way today. I've had heart surgery so I have to get my exercise. Beautiful, isn't it?"

We stopped and gazed out over the hills, at the cypresses and the palms and the sky just beginning to turn pink.

"Beautiful," I agreed.

"This time of year..." he said. "There's a reason they call it the Golden State."

I extended my hands, palms up, as if to embrace the whole world.

"We love LA" I summarized.

Such serendipitous moments of communion, to me, are some of the sweetest fruit of the contemplative life.

And all the way down the hill to church, I thought: *That was Christ. I just ran into Christ.*

SLOW-ROASTED SHOULDER OF PORK

I'm no vegetarian. I love a couple of pieces of bacon, a few slices of salami, an occasional cheeseburger, and, every so often, a giant mess of spareribs.

But as you can see, I am not a huge cooker of meat. In general, I just don't know meat. I don't know the cuts, I don't know what to do with it. Don't get me wrong: my friend Brian made prime rib recently and I swooned. But more than a few times a year, an enormous helping of meat strikes me as faintly gross. I don't mean in a save-the-animals way—every time I pass a homeless guy I think, *Let's start an organization called PETP: People for the Ethical Treatment of People*—though kindness to animals and good stewardship of the environment are definitely considerations. I mean aesthetically. If you believe, as Dostoevsky said, that "The world will be saved by beauty," you'll live in such a way that you automatically feel distaste at the prospect of making a hog out of yourself—in *any* way.

Still, let's say one of these "few times a year" has arrived: have I got the dish for you. I served this once to a *Cuban* and she said the pork was the best she'd ever had.

I found pork shoulder butt easily in the meat department of the nearest ordinary grocery store. The guy said "picnic" (another cut) was the same thing and who am I to argue? Also, the recipe calls for boneless but when boneless wasn't available I've used bone-in a couple of times and the meat turned out fine.

The thrilling thing about this dish is the ten and a half hours roasting time. That's right. TEN AND A HALF HOURS. At that point, sticking a serving fork into the meat is like putting a knife into room temperature butter. You'll be bowled over by the tenderness.

Plus, the house—actually, the block—will smell tantalizingly of fennel seeds, garlic, chiles, and roasted, almost caramelized meat.

INGREDIENTS

10 garlic cloves, peeled
½ cup fennel seeds
2 tablespoons coarse sea salt
½ teaspoon freshly ground black pepper
5–6 small dried red chiles, crumbled, with seeds

1 boneless pork shoulder butt (about 6–7 pounds)
4 tablespoons olive oil, divided
½ cup hot water
Juice of 1 lemon
½ cup chicken broth

TO PREPARE

1. Heat oven to 450 degrees. Using a mortar and pestle, crush the garlic and fennel seeds and mix them together. Add the salt, pepper, and chiles and combine.
2. Cut 1-inch slits all over the surface of the meat, including top and bottom. Rub the garlic-seed mixture into the slits.
3. Heat 2 tablespoons olive oil in a large, heavy dutch oven. Sear the meat on all sides over medium-low heat for about 10–12 minutes. Do not allow the garlic to burn.
4. Remove the roast from the pot and add the hot water, stirring and scraping the bottom to deglaze the pan. Place a rack in the bottom of the pan. Add the meat, fatty side up, and roast in the oven uncovered for 30 minutes.
5. Pour the lemon juice and the chicken broth over the meat. Brush with the remaining olive oil.
6. Reduce the heat to 250 degrees, cover the pan and roast the meat 8–10 hours, occasionally basting with pan juices. The roast will be done when the meat falls apart when barely touched with a fork.
7. Remove the roast from the pot and place it on a serving platter. Skim the fat from the pan drippings. Serve pan drippings on the side or drizzled over the meat.

⮞ 21 ⮜

Fast, Pray, Love

Several years ago, legions of thirty-something gals read *Eat, Pray, Love* and signed on for Bali. All I could think was that any spiritual seeker worth his or her salt has undertaken a journey so full of failure, hardship, and disappointment that *noone* would want to follow it.

Does anyone *really* want to follow in the footsteps of Simone Weil, or Martin Luther King Jr., or Christ? I can't think of anything creepier than someone trying to literally retrace the path of another, hoping for the same "happy ending" result. Tip: there are no happy endings, not any we try to engineer for ourselves anyway. Let's carve out our own path. Let's each undertake our own desert journey.

Catherine de Hueck Doherty was a Russian whose journey as an exiled émigré took her to Ontario, Canada, where she founded a lay community called Madonna House, worked with the poor, and wrote prolifically.

In *Poustinia: Christian Spirituality of the East for Western Man*, she observed of the difficulty of community life:

> As you know only too well, the divisions, arguments, and power plays that take place at meetings witness to the fragmentation of humanity. By your presence in love, you have to witness to how much time is wasted, how much selfishness is going on, how much greed *there is for power, attention, and recognition....* If by prayer you have received food from God, you should be able, at these meetings, to give the oil of tenderness and the wine of

compassion, first to each other, and then to everyone you meet. All this is done silently, in the secret places of your hearts.

An incident from the life of [cofounder of the lay Catholic Worker movement] Dorothy Day expresses well what I am trying to say here. Dorothy went to Rome during the [Second Vatican] Council. Several years later when I met her in Rome I asked her what she did during the time the Council was in session. She said she had simply taken a room in the poor quarter of the city, and for ten days she fasted on bread and water and prayed for the Council. That was all she did! Then she returned to New York the way she had come—on a freight boat! Maybe this was the reason why the Council was so successful. In the eyes of God, who knows?"

That's eating. That's praying. That's love.

BULGUR AND LENTIL PILAF WITH CARAMELIZED ONIONS

Back when I got breast cancer in 2000, I started a (what turned out to be rather lackluster) campaign to reduce the fat in my diet. It was around that time that I discovered cookbook writer Paula Wolfert. Paula would travel to the Mideast, track down some ancient granny in a black headscarf, and follow her out to the shores of the Aegean. There, the ancient crone would gather bunches of fragrant wild sorrel in her homespun muslin apron, strike two twigs together, start a fire on a rough stone, and produce on the spot a round of sun-warmed, herb-flecked flatbread.

I'm a sucker for that sort of thing and for a few years I was constantly scouring the aisles of the local Armenian markets for wheat berries, pomegranate molasses, rose water, black currant juice, and various grades of couscous.

Mediterranean Grains and Greens was the Wolfert book I liked best, but *The Cooking of the Eastern Mediterranean* was a close second.

The latter contains a recipe that, adapted, I made frequently. It calls for black lentils but I used the brown ones that were usually on hand. This makes for a uniform yellow-brown mass that if not *the* most visually exciting dish ever is nonetheless addictively delicious. I always left out the tomato paste and red pepper paste—the addition of which would also make for a sprightlier visual—and would instead throw in a tablespoon or so of red pepper flakes.

As long as you stick to the liquid/pasta, rice, or bean ratio, you really can't miss. And let's not forget: a giant mound of caramelized onions makes just about anything taste good.

INGREDIENTS

1 cup black lentils
3½ cups, plus or minus, chicken, meat, or vegetable stock
3 tablespoons butter (Paula calls for clarified but I always use regular)
3 tablespoons olive oil
5 medium onions, peeled and thinly sliced
2 cups coarse-grain bulgur
Sea salt
1 tablespoon tomato paste
1 tablespoon red pepper paste
Freshly ground black pepper
½ teaspoon Near East pepper or
¼ teaspoon crushed red pepper flakes

TO PREPARE

1. Boil the lentils in three cups of water until tender. Add enough stock to the remaining liquor, if any, to make 3½ cups and set aside.
2. Meanwhile, heat the butter and oil in a large sauté pan and cook the thinly sliced onions over medium to medium-low heat, stirring frequently, until a deep caramelized brown.
3. In a heavy stockpot or saucepan, place the bulgur, lentils, salt, tomato paste, pepper paste, and stock and bring to a boil. Reduce to low and cook, covered, for 15 minutes. Place a paper towel (why? I don't know but it's fun) over the bulgur mixture, cover the pan, and let sit over a flame tamer, or over very low heat, to cook for another 10 minutes. Cool slightly.
4. Add several grindings of fresh black pepper and the Near East pepper (or crushed red pepper flakes) to the caramelized onions and bring to a sizzle. Pour over the bulgur, stir gently, pour into your favorite decorative bowl, and serve.

As Paula says, "With thanks to Mrs. Filiz Hösukoğlu for sharing this recipe."

⇒ 22 ⇐

Reality Food

"There's nothing as cozy as a piece of candy and a book."

—Betty MacDonald

I have never seen a reality show but I've heard tell of them, in particular a series called *Iron Chef* that, according to Wikipedia, consists of "a timed cooking battle built around a specific theme ingredient." A battle? *Timed?* Around food? The purpose of food is to bring us together, not pit us against each other as adversaries. And just because you can accomplish a particular task in a frenzied rush doesn't mean you should. How about Iron Surgeon, Iron Lend-a-Compassinate-Ear-to-Your-Friend-Who's-Just-Found-Out-Her-Husband-is-Cheating-On-Her, Iron Sleep?

Here are three "recipes" I've worked up over the last few weeks that in one sense don't take a lot of time, and in another sense take a lifetime.

1. Take a piece of Celebrity Healthy Ham from Trader Joe's and roll crosswise into a spiral. Dip directly into a large jar of mayonnaise and eat, bite by mayonnaise-dipped bite, while thoughtfully gazing at the bare stucco wall of the house next door and admiring the olive-green trim around the windows.

2. Walk down Sunset Boulevard in a light drizzle of rain to the 99 Cents Only Store and buy two tubes of Pepsodent, a package of votive candles, and, on a whim, a 76-cent frozen chicken pot pie. Bring the chicken pot pie home, enjoying the smell of wet wild fennel and the

sound of tires on wet pavement and the feel of the rain on your face, and put it in a 375-degree oven. While it's cooking, think of similarly evocative childhood treats: Campbell's cream of mushroom soup, lobster newburg (the lobster from your father's traps), your mother's homemade popovers. Eat with a teaspoon, in bed, scraping the last bits of crust from the tinfoil, while reading Camus' *The Plague.*

3. Take your friend Glenn, who just had a hip replacement, to the Saturday vigil Mass at St. Basil's. Yield to his offer to take you for udon at the tiny stall/café at the back of Assi on Oxford and 8th. Afterward, troll the aisles and come upon an item called Buenas Fruit Mix and Beans Halo-Halo, a glass jar containing red mung beans, coconut gel, palm fruit, jackfruit, macapuno, white beans, and sodium hydrogen sulphite, the main ingredient of which, however, is pure cane sugar.

   Let that pure cane sugar recommend itself to you. Shell out a buck ninety-nine, wait with Glenn in the parking lot for the AAA guy because you had to take Glenn's car (the seat in your Celica was too low for his injured hip) and it somehow broke down while you were in Assi, accompany him home, retrieve your own car, and drive you and your precious jar home.

   While still in your coat, take a quart container of French Village plain yogurt, also from Trader Joe's (the kind with about a third of an inch of heavy cream on the top) from the fridge. Remove the gold-and-blue glazed Provence cup (the one you bought on Boston's Newbury Street) from the dish drainer. Put a ton of yogurt in the cup, then add a couple of giant spoonfuls of halo-halo and stir.

   Bring it to the room where you eat. Take off your coat. Check your email. See that, one more time, nothing's come over the transom even remotely promising money, sex, or fame.

   Close your eyes. Give thanks for your health, your friends, your car, and that you had a buck ninety-nine.

RED AND GOLDEN BEETS WITH BLOOD ORANGES, ENDIVE, AND WALNUTS

Candy's good, ham dipped in mayo is good, frozen chicken pot pies are good, but then it's time for something solid, interesting, and substantial.

This is another recipe that's been in my file box for ages: tried, true, inexpensive yet classy, and with those blood oranges, a jolt of spring passion. I was never crazy about beets until I learned how to roast them in the oven, and that they are delicious with goat cheese and/or citrus and/or nuts. The pale green endive, red-gold oranges, citrus vinaigrette, and deep purple and golden beets pair beautifully visually as well.

INGREDIENTS

2 pounds red and golden beets
½ cup shelled walnuts
2 blood or navel oranges
2 tablespoons red wine vinegar
2 tablespoons orange juice
Zest of ½ orange, finely chopped
¼ cup olive oil
Salt, pepper
¼ pound belgian endive

TO PREPARE

1. Heat the oven to 400 degrees. Trim and wash the beets and roast them, tightly covered, with a splash of water in a roasting pan until very tender, 50–60 minutes.

2. While the oven is on, place the walnuts on a baking sheet and toast them about 5 minutes. With a sharp paring knife, trim off the top and bottom of each orange. Pare off the rest of the peel, making sure to remove all of the pith. Slice the oranges into quarter inch rounds.

3. Make a vinaigrette by mixing together the vinegar, orange juice, and the zest, and stirring in the olive oil and salt and pepper to taste.

4. When the beets are cool enough to handle, peel them and slice into rounds. Toss them gently with the vinaigrette and arrange the beets on a plate with the orange slices and belgian endive leaves. Drizzle over any vinaigrette remaining in the bowl, and garnish with the toasted walnuts.

≫ 23 ≪

The Miracle of the Loaves and Fishes: On Being a Host

My ideal way to cook is an elaborate meal for eight with one or two more recipes, several more ingredients, and the necessity of shopping at way more stores than is entirely sane.

From the working out of the menu to full cleanup, it's a two-day (at least) extravaganza. Inevitably, I have to drive across town for duck confit; make a detour to the mom-and-pop Indian store for chickpea flour; or run out to the street at the last minute to filch a sprig of rosemary from a bush on the median strip. Inevitably, one ingredient—flageolets, kumquats, verjus—is out of season or impossible to find. (Other typical challenges include the recipe with an unfamiliar cooking method (baking en papillote, for example, or anything involving a candy thermometer); the meal with an entrée I've never made before, like oxtails or bisteeya; and the dinner with guests from different parts of my life who I'm terrified will antagonize each another).

A typical menu (this one courtesy of Suzanne Goin's *Sunday Suppers at Lucques*) might start with Endive Salad with Meyer Lemon, Fava Beans and Oil-Cured Olives. (A word here about Meyer lemons, one of Southern California's finest treasures: thin-skinned, ultra juicy, less sharp than the thick-skinned lemons at the supermarket, and a luscious deep orange-gold with smooth velvety skin. We had a tree in the back of my K-town apartment complex and from December to May, when Meyers are in season, I didn't buy lemons for years. They probably don't travel well, which is why you seldom see them in the supermarkets, even in Southern California).

Then I might move on to Beets and Tangerines with Mint and Orange-Flower Water, Orecchiette with Cauliflower, Cavalo Nero, Currants and Pine Nuts (this includes a sub-recipe of Currant and Pine Nut Relish), Mustard Grilled Chicken with Fennel, Roasted Shallots and Mustard Greens, and Olive Oil Cake with Crème Fraîche and Candied Tangerines. Preparing a meal like that is a little like an extreme sport. The shopping in this case involved trips to Trader Joe's, the 99 Cents Only Store, and the Silver Lake Farmers Market. I held my breath for the fresh fava beans, which can be hard to find, but Jons (a chain of Armenian markets) came through (as it did for the fresh tarragon, chives, thyme; currants (always tricky); and orange-flower water).

There's the hauling in and the putting away of the groceries. And then there's the sheer labor of cooking: the chopping of fennel, shallots, garlic, herbs, beets; the peeling and pithing of tangerines; the grating of lemons; the whisking of dressings; the mixing of batter; the sautéing, baking, poaching, broiling; the rapidly growing piles of dishes, the attempt to clean up as I go along.

I'm on my feet all day: juggling fifty different tasks, carrying a huge amount of tension, never quite knowing if everything's going to come together. On top of it, I have to clean the house, make sure there's enough ice, cold drinks, butter, napkins, plates, chairs. Put out flowers. Decide whether I want to have music, and if so, what kind. Make sure the bathroom is clean. Change into something besides jeans and a frayed T-shirt stained with olive oil and nutmeg.

Just when I'm ready to collapse, I get to put on my hostess hat! Be a hostess!

Speaking of which, with my friends, actually, the major challenge is nailing down enough people to even make a dinner "party." One is likely to be in the grip of agoraphobia, another can't afford gas, a third has been holed up for weeks working on a screenplay and refuses to be coaxed from her lair. Two others are sure to be fighting, and another will inevitably be on a cleanse, raw food kick, or honey-and-maple-syrup fast.

The night in question, I'd managed to round up Ron, who used to be the film editor for the *LA Weekly* and has watched all 121 episodes of

Lost three times; Dave, a sculptor who lives in a tiny studio, rides the bus, and is working on a book called *Freeway*; Donald, a healthcare advocate and massage therapist who brought five fat pomegranates from the tree in his yard; Maudie, a visual artist who'd composed a delicious salad with radicchio, basil, and mint; and Terry, a writer, who showed up with a bouquet of feathery greens, small blue wildflowers, and branches of small oval leaves edged in cream, all picked from the grounds of her apartment complex and beautifully arranged in an oblong glass pitcher.

Dave turned out to be a grillmeister, which was lucky, as I thrust the chicken at him as soon as he arrived and it came out perfectly, whereas I would have either burnt it to a crisp or served it semi-raw.

I'm no good at garnishing nor presentation and, as I always do, had to ask someone (in this case Maudie) to help. Still, the food was great. Everyone got along famously. Lacking an electric beater, I arrived at the dinner table post-meal with a bowl of heavy cream and a hand beater, plunked both into the hands of the nearest guest, brayed, "Pass it around! *You* all do it," and repaired to the kitchen to nibble leftovers and make coffee, which pretty much emblemizes my hostess zeitgeist.

The Postmortem—that particular night conducted by Donald, Dave, and me—is an essential, if not the very best part of, the whole meal

There's food and then there's food. And when we feed others, we get fed, too.

TAPENADE (ANCHOVY-OLIVE APPETIZER)

No matter how things shake out, somehow at every dinner party I throw, this tapenade (I use the term loosely) makes an appearance. It's sharp and rich, with a hint of heat, and thus whets the appetite and stimulates thirst. I don't know about you, but the sight of a bowl of coarsely chopped black oil-cured olives, slices of lemon, flecks of red pepper, and a piece of stray bay leaf makes my heart sing.

This is another dish you can hardly wreck, and making it couldn't be easier. When I'm crushing those pine nuts with the side of a big knife, I know the dinner party has begun—even if the guests won't arrive for hours.

INGREDIENTS

1 pound olives (mix Greek kalamatas, French picholine, and Morocan wrinkled, or
another combination, or blacks and greens)
2 tablespoons pine nuts
4 anchovy fillets, minced
3 bay leaves
⅛ teaspoon crushed red pepper
½ lemon thinly sliced
¼ cup olive oil

TO PREPARE

1. Pit and coarsely chop the olives.
2. Mash one tablespoon of the pine nuts and leave the rest whole.
3. Combine all the ingredients in a serving dish and let stand at room temperature for one hour.
4. Serve with raw vegetables, crackers, breadsticks, or lots of Italian bread to mop up the oil.

≥ 24 ≤

Hard Times/Good Times

The other morning in the shower, suddenly I thought: *I bet the people who read my books wonder what I eat.* No? Well, I'm gonna tell ya anyway: tuscan kale and pasta.

I don't mean every meal! That would leave no room for the Spoon Size Shredded Wheat and raisins or single poached egg on toast for breakfast, nor the salad of spring mix and shaved carrots for lunch, nor the tonnage of dried sweetened mango, roasted almonds, Ak-Mak crackers, French Village Plain Cream Line Yogurt, cheese, and coffee that sustain me for the rest of the day.

I just mean four or five meals a week, if I get to the Silver Lake Farmer's Market on Saturday, that is, where I purchase a couple of bunches of greens: maybe that Hmong rapini lookalike with yellow flowers ($1), maybe a tuscan kale ($1.50). And then Monday (and Wednesday or Thursday) afternoon around 2, after I have feverishly written all morning, working myself into a state of catatonic excitement and/or despair, I proceed as follows—in a way you may or may not be moved to get on board with, too.

First you put on the water for the pasta and cut the greens, just three slashes with a big knife and throw them into a frying pan in which you've heated a generous amount of olive oil and sauté them over fairly high heat till they start to almost burn a bit. Then you throw on a third or so of a coffee cup of water and put your housemate's screen thing over the top 'cause the oil will splatter. Meanwhile, you mince up a couple of cloves of garlic and three or four anchovies. Now, if you're one of those people who when you hear the word "anchovy," respond ECCCHHHH, I will still be your friend, but I really don't know what to say other than that I'll pray for you.

Then you throw in a third of a package or so of linguine or fettuccine or penne and, after the water's all absorbed from the sauté pan, shove the greens up aside against the far side, heat an additional small puddle of olive oil and sauté the garlic and anchovies, mashing up the latter. (You can add some dried hot red pepper here as well. The Chez Panisse recipe referenced below incorporates red wine vinegar, too, but I don't).

Drain the pasta, put a giant serving in a big bowl, add a little butter, heap on some greens, salt, ground pepper, and if you're feeling flush, which I, for one, have definitely not as of late, grate over some real Parmigiano-Reggiano and if not, sprinkle over some of the vastly inferior but not entirely grotesque shaved parmesan-romano-asiago mixture from Trader Joe's, and Bob's your uncle.

Afterward, I like to take a nice long walk around the hilly streets of Silver Lake, pondering God's infinite bounty and the unsolvable problems of life, heart, and writing that cropped up that day.

In this way, I keep my food bill down to approximately $23.87 a week, leaving lots of spare change for the Sunset Boulevard panhandlers, drunks, and psychotics who brighten my existence.

Bon appétit!

CHEZ PANISSE SAUTÉED GREENS

As you may know, Chez Panisse is the Berkeley restaurant founded by Alice Waters, California doyenne of all that is fresh, green, local, organic and heirloom.

My copy of the *Chez Panisse Café Cookbook* is smeared with chocolate, extra virgin olive oil, and dried egg white.

Some of it's a bit precious—Wild Mushroom Pasta Handkerchiefs, Peach Leaf Crème Brûlée—but the thirty-four bucks would have been well spent even if I'd taken away nothing more than a single recipe: Spicy Broccoli Raab, from which the above way of cooking tuscan kale was derived.

Check out the cookbook or one of the many others Waters has written. Just reading about the food will cheer you up—even if you never make or eat any of it. Thank you, Alice!

⇒ 25 ⇐

The Prodigal Daughter and the Banquet Table

An interview with Elizabeth Scalia, author, blogger, and editor in chief of Aleteia [aleteia.org]. The subject was my book, *Shirt of Flame: A Year with St. Thérèse of Lisieux.*

Thérèse wrote under obedience. You sort of write under obedience, too, don't you?

In a sense, yes. I am not affiliated with any movement, organization, cause, politics, or institution other than the Church. But that "other than the Church" is key. Without the Church, I am nothing. My "authority" is Christ; my authority is my heart.

I was trained as a lawyer and a big part of my search consisted in having "achieved" what supposedly constitutes the American dream and discovering that that particular version of the dream was killing me. I want to emphasize that lawyering is absolutely the call of someone *else's* heart. But it wasn't the call of mine, and I underwent a major spiritual crisis that consisted of trying to discern God's will for me and discovering, as many of us do if we're lucky, that God does not "want" us to do the grim, hard thing. He wants us to do the absorbing, exciting, "come-higher-friend" hard thing, which turns out to be exactly what we want, too.

So I quit my job, embarked upon the precarious life of a freelance writer, and eighteen years of blood, sweat, tears and three books later, I just received a comment on my blog saying, "I've always thought you were a bit self-absorbed but I see you're beginning to move away from that. Good work!" Part of me wanted to laugh and part of me wanted to cry. "Don't hold your breath if you're waiting for *me* to stop being self-absorbed!" I wanted to tell the guy. I thought back over the years and years of more or less solitary pilgrimage, of sleeping alone, of pondering. Of writing week in, week out for what amounts to about minimum wage. Of spending five, six, eight hours on a single (unpaid) blog post because I so want to get it right; I so want to impart this crazy, improbably joy in the midst of sorrow I've stumbled upon.

And in the end I get a crumb of dubious praise from some guy who's sitting in an air-conditioned office playing solitaire and tossing off random blog comments. Truly, God has a sense of humor. Because what I really get is the opportunity to be more vulnerable, to be more teachable, more responsible. What I get in return is life as a kind of *poustinia*. The door of my little hut is always open and people are always coming in, with questions, insights, arguments; the need for solace, comfort, thanks, understanding; requests for prayer. I spend at least an hour or two a day responding, with as much love and patience as I can muster, to emails, and I also somehow make enough money to live on, and I also know this is the joy and height and depth and fullness and glory of my life and I would not trade one second of it for anything on earth.

I have to live with the terrible tension of my bottomless imperfection, weakness, self-righteousness and pride and to believe that my task is to write anyway. And at the same time, I have to be constantly discerning. There may come a time to fall silent for awhile. Because the danger for me in writing and speaking is a lack of prayer; that my prayer life falls away or suffers. I'm very careful to work a lot of silence and solitude into my life, but even the silence can become tinged with anxiety about "work." The impetus for the work has in some sense to be my conviction that what I have to say is important and that no-one else is saying it, or saying it quite the way I do. And therein lies the danger as well.

At the end of his life St. Thomas Aquinas regarded his gigantic *oeuvre* and said "All straw." Later, Christ appeared to him in a vision and said, in effect, "Good job, my son! Tell me your greatest wish and I will grant it. What wouldst thou have?" St. Thomas replied, *Nil nisi te* (Nothing but Thee). In the end, no matter how much or how well or how truly I write, the only possible account I will be able to give of myself is that I have been to Mass. I have participated in the Eucharist and I have tried to take Christ's Body and Blood out into the world and share it there. I have loved Him as best I can to the limit of my heart, mind, soul, and strength. So yes, obedience, which actually means "to listen carefully." Continuing obedience.

In the book, you describe a kind of Incarnational Mysticism—the grace of doing everything for God, and seeing everything as coming from God. Without grace, this would seem impossible. Our faulty humanity would constantly distract us, challenge us, get in the way. But is this something one can train oneself to do? Because it seems to me if one could, it would remove every obstacle to peace.

Well, I think the grace is a completely unbidden, unmerited gift and then, as has often been said, we get to cooperate with it. I got the grace of having the obsession to drink removed, for one central example, and for twenty-seven years I've devoted ten or twelve hours a week to cooperating. Directly cooperating with that particular grace, and then there are the many, many more hours when I cooperate with grace in general. I am fairly disciplined, which stems in part from my desperate need to manage and control, but make your neuroses work for you, I say! And to be fair, I've simply seen that some kind of rudimentary discipline—which is itself a grace—works. "Moving easy in harness" Robert Frost described the rules of poetry, and once the harness is in place you find you're being guided where you wanted to go, perhaps unbeknownst to yourself, all along.

I try to pray the Office each morning, I write in my journal, I work, I take a walk, I run things by a spiritual director, I often go to daily Mass, or sit before the Blessed Sacrament. I avail myself of the Sacrament of Reconciliation. All that has absolutely formed me. But the discipline is just tilling the ground so I can receive the gift; so the seed can bear fruit. I think that's what you discover on the spiritual path. It is ALL gift. It is ALL grace. We take up our cross—and what I've learned is that the cross is basically myself—but just as Christ said, the gift we receive is to live fully and in abundant joy—even as we're suffering. Christianity is about our daily lives, our lives today, a whole way of looking at and experiencing the world. It's about interior freedom. It's about human relationship.

That said, no amount of training or discipline in and of itself leads to peace. Letting go of every old idea we have about how we're going to fix ourselves leads to peace. Dying to our identities as "good" people, righteous people, people who need to establish our supremacy, people who need to be perfect, people who need to have all the loose ends tied up, leads to peace. Dying to the notion that we need to do anything but open ourselves to God's inexhaustible love leads to peace. Reminding ourselves that we are not one whit better, more advanced, or different than any other human being on earth leads to peace.

I wrote a series of posts not long ago on nonviolence as the chief characteristic of God's love for us; nonviolence as the mystical phenomenon/dynamic that underlies all of existence. I was very careful to emphasize that I wasn't talking about nonviolence as a political theory but a mystical phenomenon, starting with our violence toward ourselves. And I was staggered by the number of people who came out jabbing their finger at the Catechism and saying "Unh, EXCUSE me, it says right here we have the right to defend ourselves! What are we supposed to just stand by and let our children be raped and cut up into tiny little pieces? What are we supposed to just let the Japanese attack us at Pearl Harbor? What are we supposed to just let Hitler...? Why, the *just war* theory. So you know these people are suffering terribly and that they can't see that by denying mercy to others, they deny it to themselves. And by "they" I of course mean myself as well. In a sense, our inability to love ourselves is my/your/our central problem.

Still, I want to say, Oh if only you were an alcoholic and were able to hit some terrible bottom, if only you were in touch enough with your own thirst that you squandered your whole inheritance in the mire and then came home again and found the table had been laid! I think that's why Christ said "Blessed are the poor in spirit," because it's been a great grace to be so in touch with my own brokenness, so badly in need of mercy—and then to have found that the mercy is there! The mercy is there even if we don't ask for it! The mercy is there even if we don't know what mercy is! The mercy is there *entirely apart from us "deserving" it!* That is the very nature of mercy, of love. And then our feeling becomes—Oh who wants to fight? Who cares about building up arms? Let's eat together! Let's have a meal and listen to some music together! Let's sit around the table together and break bread and tell stories!

You don't disregard the problems of the world; you joyfully participate in the sorrows of the world.

I came into the Church as a sinner, and I remain as a sinner—a Prodigal Daughter, forever invited to the banquet table. Now *that's* grace.

QUINOA SALAD WITH GRILLED SCALLIONS, FAVAS, AND DATES

A couple of winters ago a friend gave me four two-pound bags of basmati brown rice, a huge bag of adzuki beans, and a pound of quinoa. I can't quite remember why, or maybe there was no particular reason, but right away I started calculating how to use all that starch up.

It was my first introduction to quinoa, which I'd always thought was pronounced the way it's spelled: quinn-OH-ah. Imagine my surprise when I learned quinoa was the KEEN-wah I'd heard people blathering about! Anyway, quinoa looks and tastes like teeny teeny Styrofoam balls, which is not necessarily a bad thing. I'd cook half a cup at a time, lard with raisins, mix in some milk and brown sugar, and have a bowl for breakfast. The rest sat in the cupboard for months. Bothering me. My anti-wastage OCD means I can never have a bunch of foodstuffs simply languishing about the kitchen. Eventually, I have to find a way to use every last quarter cup of dried cranberries, drop of almond extract, and, to the point here, quinoa, even if it means spending ten bucks on more ingredients. That will in turn transform into leftovers, and form the basis of the next guilt trip.

So I started googling quinoa recipes and almost immediately, this one came up. The sound of grilled dates in particular fired my imagination. Grilled dates! I could just stick them with a fork and hold them over the gas burner! Which was a blast: food and open fire are a natural match, and the dates softened inside and charred on the outside quickly.

While making a mess (in my roommate's kitchen: she was gone) with the dates, I found a nifty contraption in the drawer beneath the stove that I eventually grasped had been designed for this very purpose, grilling stovetop over an open flame—a kind of shallow wire cage that fit over the burners and across which I then lay my scallions, leeks and what we call in these part Mexican onions, which are like scallions except with a much bigger bulb. Fava beans were out of season, so I thawed some edamame from Trader Joe's and threw them in sans grilling and they worked fine.

Grilled dates, fava beans, and spring onions would make actual Styrofoam taste good and, with quinoa, they were divine. I served this (among other things) with Slow-Roasted Shoulder of Pork (recipe several chapters above) for a friend's birthday party and am still recovering from the beauty.

With thanks to chef Charlie Parker, from whom the recipe is adapted.

INGREDIENTS

1 cup red quinoa, rinsed (I used the bag I had on hand, which was light brown)
2 cups water
8 soft medjool dates, pitted
2 tablespoons sherry vinegar
Salt
1 pound fava beans in the pod
Finely grated zest and juice of 1 lemon
1/3 cup extra-virgin olive oil
Freshly ground pepper
12 scallions
6 stalks of green garlic or baby leeks
2 tablespoons chopped mint
1 cup small sorrel or arugula leaves

TO PREPARE

1. Measure the quinoa into a pot, cover with water, and bring to a boil. Cover and cook over low to medium heat until the water has been absorbed and the quinoa is tender, 15 minutes or so. Uncover, fluff the quinoa, and transfer to a large bowl.
2. Meanwhile, light a grill (or a burner on your gas stove). Grill the dates over moderate heat until lightly charred and very soft. If you spear them with a fork and hold them to the flame this will take less than 30 seconds; otherwise, grill for a couple of minutes. Transfer the dates to a bowl and mash to a purée with a fork. Mine didn't mash that well so I cut them up into smallish chunks. Stir in the vinegar and season the date mixture with salt.
3. Grill the fava bean pods over moderately high heat, turning, until the pods are softened and hot within, about 5 minutes. Transfer the pods to a bowl, cover with foil and let steam for 5 minutes. (Or as I said, use

edamame, fresh or frozen, and skip this step of the grilling).

4. In a small bowl, stir the lemon zest, juice, and olive oil and season with salt and pepper. Shell and peel the fava beans and toss them with 1 tablespoon of the dressing.

5. Brush the scallions and green garlic with some of the dressing, season with salt and pepper, and grill over moderately high heat, turning, until browned and tender, about 2 minutes. When done, cut into 2-inch lengths.

6. Mix the fava beans, scallions, green garlic, and mint into the quinoa. Add the remaining dressing and toss well. Season with salt and pepper. At this point, I threw in the date purée and arugula, mixed it all together and served.

7. But if you want to get fancy, you can spread the date purée/mixture on the bottoms of 4 plates, spoon the quinoa salad on top, garnish with the arugula or sorrel leaves, and serve that way. (Presentation is not my forte: not bragging.)

Note: The quinoa can be cooked ahead and refrigerated overnight.

≋ 26 ≋

The Driveway Garden:
On Being a Guest

My friend Brian grew up in the tiny town of Roseau, Minnesota (current pop. 2,800), six miles from the Canadian border. His parents, Charleen and Ardmore, farmed 1,200 acres of wheat, soybeans, canola, barley, and flax.

Now he lives in West Hollywood, goes on auditions, and does makeup and hair (one of his clients was Mariah Carey).

He's showed me photos of his homeland, though picturing Brian on a farm is difficult.

"So do you help out when you go back?" I ask eagerly. "Can you drive a tractor?"

"Hell, yeah! I grew up on a tractor."

Growing up in a home with a mother so frugal she had the same one apron, pot holder, and can of turmeric for forty years, I'm fascinated by other people's kitchens, and love snooping around looking for personality clues: hoarders, clutterers, collectors of beautiful (which doesn't necessarily mean expensive) plates and bowls.

Of course there are other kinds of clues to be found in and around people's kitchens. People who make you wait three hours before eating. People who don't offer you even a glass of water. I don't care if you offer me a glass of tap water in a Flintstones glass and a saltine: I will relish both if I'm hungry and thirsty enough, and in any case I will feel the welcome, the hospitality. I think you can evaluate a person's entire character by the way they welcome you. The person who can meet you at the door, look you in the eye with warmth, offer you a seat at the table, and say, "Tell me about yourself" with genuine interest—that, to me, is a human being.

The other night, Brian invited me and some other friends to dinner. I arrived a bit early to find him dashing about the kitchen in that oh-my-God-people-are-going-to-be-here-soon-and-I-haven't-even-started-the-sauce-gribiche state that, having given dinner parties myself, I knew all too well.

He was wearing a T-Shirt that read "Bring Back the Beet" and what looked like a scary black oilcloth butcher apron but turned out to be part of the garb he dons in his capacity as developer, CEO, president, and head beautician/magician of Makeover Workshop.

"Check out this celery," he said, handing me a bunch topped by the deep green leaves, the stalks as slender as a ballet dancer's waist.

"Wow, beautiful—did you go to the Farmers Market today?"

"No, I grew it."

"You grew your own *celery*!" I'd seen the strawberry patch, the basil, rosemary, sage, thyme, and heirloom tomatoes by his front door, but I had no idea he had a back garden. "What, you have a plot by the garage?" I asked.

"Kind of," he said, washing a head of butter lettuce. "I plant stuff all along the driveway. Hey, can you peel these beets?"

I peeled beets and snooped through the cupboards (one shelf was stacked high with cardboard packs of hair color). The other guests arrived. We exchanged news, we made fun of each other, we pushed aside the display cases of makeup, sat down, said grace, and ate.

We had oven-braised baby carrots in rich hues of orange, gold, and deep red.

We had avocado and roasted beet salad with citrus dressing.

We had chicken with warm bread salad and watercress from the Zuni Café cookbook (when he lived in San Francisco, Brian waited tables there).

We had four or five different vegetables and Brian had grown every one of them.

We had coffee and Tom's delicious chocolate mousse with cardamom, we gossiped and gabbed, we did the dishes, and when it was almost eleven, Brian strapped on a headlamp and said, "Come on, I'll show you the garden."

So out the other guests and I trooped, and there, hard by congested Santa Monica Boulevard, in notoriously cramped, impossible-to-find-parking West Hollywood, Brian, it turned out, had managed to create a fourteen-inch wide plot, backed by a cinder block wall, that ran the whole length of the lot-long driveway.

"LA has sun. The problem," he explained, gesturing to the adjacent three-story apartment complex, "is that the buildings block it out. Right here actually gets the best sun anywhere on the property, especially up by the garages where the house isn't in the way. At first I thought such a narrow strip would be constraining, but the asphalt gives me a place to stand so I don't have to wade through the mud. The driveway makes a natural border. And I can plant small sections that turn out to be convenient to tend and pick from."

He grows curly kale, russian kale, and tuscan kale; red beets, golden beets and chioggia beets. He grows butter lettuce, speckled lettuce, watercress, brussel sprouts, romaine, arugula, and carrots.

"How do you water it?" someone asked.

"Out of consideration for my neighbors—and because the water pressure out here is almost nil—by hand. In the middle of the summer I've hauled out twenty-five buckets of water a day, one by one."

How often in LA, or anywhere, do you get a meal in which every dish has not only been cooked by scratch, but where the cook has personally planted, hand-watered, and picked the vegetables?

"Want some arugula?" Brian asked, tearing off a good-sized bunch. Then this hairdresser to the stars straightened up, gazed thoughtfully at the sky, and said, "There's a cold trough coming in from Alaska. I can feel it."

He hopes to visit Roseau later in the spring.

PEACH KUCHEN

Adapted from *The Tassajara Bread Book*

I came of cooking age in the '70s, and *The Tassajara Bread Book* was one of my bibles. I can see it now: the homespun brown paper cover (I'm talking the 1969 version) that you just knew some Buddhist monk had fashioned from garden-grown hemp and a centuries-old Japanese paper press; the line drawings that had the same feel as the album cover for Joni Mitchell's *Ladies of the Canyon*. For years O-Konomi-Yaki and Summer Swedish Rye Bread and Cottage Cheese Pancakes from the *Tassajara* were staples in my kitchen.

But the recipe that has stayed with me all these decades later, and that I still make at least once every summer, is Peach Kuchen.

You start with a shortbread-like crust, top with halved peaches, and blanket the whole with heavy cream, eggs, and brown sugar. The peaches will look like orange-gold jewels, peeking through the beautifully browned custard. It's delicious hot or cold.

INGREDIENTS

½ cup butter
2 cups flour
¼ teaspoon baking powder
½ teaspoon salt
1 cup heavy cream or sour cream
1 cup sugar (brown or raw)
12 peach halves or 2 packages of frozen slices
2 egg yolks, beaten, or two whole eggs
1 teaspoon cinnamon or more to taste

TO PREPARE

1. Cut butter into flour, baking powder, salt, and 2 tablespoons sugar with pastry cutter, two knives, or your fingers until the mixture resembles coarse meal. Press firmly into a 9 x 12-inch baking pan.
2. Arrange peaches, round side up, on top of the pastry to cover.
3. Sprinkle fruit with a mixture of cinnamon and remaining sugar.
4. Bake 15 minutes at 400 degrees.
5. Pour egg yolks beaten with cream over top, and bake 40 minutes or longer at 375 degrees.

≥ 27 ≤

Feeding the Birds: The LA River

LA is a dream of light and motion. When the city shakes and slides and burns, we wake to remember who we are—in the foothills, along the coast, across the plains, by the river..."

—From a 2004 exhibit at the Natural History Museum of Los Angeles County entitled *LA: Light/Motion/Dreams*

Several years ago I took a guided tour of the LA River, which runs the fifty-one miles from Canoga Park to Long Beach and at the time cut a mostly unseen, mostly unremarked upon, at the time largely under-utilized swath through the city. I kept telling myself I was going to go back, but for whatever reason, I hadn't since.

Then, one afternoon last week, a friend who walks along the river frequently said, "Let's go," so we did, and I couldn't believe the lushness, the magic! The sun was shining, and a breeze was riffling the water, and all over were birds! Cormorants, egrets, mallard ducks, great blue herons. Floating, soaring, cawing, perching on rocks, skimming over the water. Also, little red crayfish with spotted claws, schools of small black darting fish, and many half-submerged, mud-covered golf balls from the nearby Los Feliz-3 Par Golf Course.

We poked sticks into the shallows and jumped over puddles and marveled over the flight of the great blues.

Just as we returned to our starting point, we came upon a little man who was feeding a giant flock of pigeons, their sleek purple-green heads forming a rippling, iridescent sea as they pecked from the ground for crumbs. Whether we startled them or the man gave a sign or St. Francis himself issued an order, as if with one mind the birds suddenly, with a majestic flapping of wings, rose, wheeled left, around and back, narrowly missing our heads, and briefly touched down. Hardly had we taken in the sight of those arrow-like bodies—regimental, balletic—performing their pigeonly maneuvers in unison, when, for good measure, they did the same thing once more.

Later I thought about how the river was like being two places at once: in the city, with the semis rolling by on the 10 above, and in the wilderness, down below with the grebes; on earth, with plastic bags snagged on the reeds, and in heaven, where the birds fly free; in time, where every afternoon eventually ends, and in eternity, where we walk—let us hope— forever with a Friend.

I went back the next night alone—vespers with the herons.

ROSEMARY CORNCAKES

This recipe comes by way of Nancy Silverton, again of LaBrea Bakery fame. The yield purports to be 12 scones but in my experience is twice that.

I'm a sucker for muffins, biscuits, and scones. Could anything be more comforting than a little hand-sized quick bread that you can eat hot or eat room temp; with butter or jam or plain? These have *a ton* of butter in them already, but I'm with the French: take smallish servings and eat what you like.

With its aromatic short glossy spears, rosemary grows so plentifully in LA that people sometimes make hedges out of it. Out walking, I often come upon a bush that out of sheer joy has rooted itself on a median strip. I sometimes nab a sprig just for the smell, and in spring its tiny purplish flowers only add to the allure. A block down from me is a primo stand that has brightened many a batch of oven-roasted potatoes, tuscan rosemary pine-nut bars, and of course, rosemary corncakes.

INGREDIENTS

3¾ cups unbleached pastry flour or unbleached all-purpose flour, plus extra for rolling out dough
1¾ cups yellow cornmeal
1 tablespoon plus ¼ teaspoon baking powder
2 teaspoons finely chopped fresh rosemary
¾ cup light brown sugar, lightly packed
1½ cups (3 sticks) unsalted butter, cut into ½-inch cubes and frozen
1 egg
1 egg yolk
2 tablespoons plus 2 teaspoons mild-flavored honey, such as clover
½ cup plus 2 teaspoons heavy cream, plus extra for brushing tops of scones
24 small tufts of fresh rosemary for garnish

TO PREPARE

1. Preheat oven to 350 degrees and line a baking sheet with parchment paper. Combine flour, cornmeal, baking powder, chopped rosemary, and brown sugar and process in a food processor or mix with an electric

beater until incorporated. Add butter and pulse a few times (or mix on low), until mixture is pale yellow and the consistency of fine meal.

2. Transfer mixture to a large bowl and make a well in the center. Pour in eggs, honey, and cream and whisk until the liquids are combined. Use your hands (fun!) to topple in the dry ingredients and mix just until combined.

3. Turn the dough out to a lightly floured work surface and gather into a ball. Pat dough into a circle about ¾ inch thick. Using a 3-inch round cutter (the top of a drinking glass, dipped in flour, works well, too), cut out scones, cutting as closely as possible and keeping the trimmings intact. Or you can cut across the big round four or five or six times and make the corncakes long triangles.

4. Gather the scraps, pat and press the pieces back together, cut scones out of the remaining dough, and repeat until dough is all used. Place scones 1 inch apart on your prepared baking sheet. Brush the tops with cream and poke 2 small tufts of rosemary into the center of each.

5. Bake until slightly browned and firm to the touch, about 30 minutes. Remove from oven and cool 5 minutes before transferring scones to a wire rack to cool.

About the Author

Heather King is a memoirist and essayist with several books, among them *Parched*; *Redeemed*; *Shirt of Flame*; *Poor Baby*; *Stumble*; *Stripped*; and *Loaded: Money and the Spirituality of Enough*. She lives in Los Angeles, speaks nationwide, appears monthly in *Magnificat*, and writes a weekly arts and culture column for *Angelus*, the archdiocesan newspaper of LA For more info and her blog, visit *Heather King: Mystery, Smarts, Laughs* (heather-king.com).

Photo by Madeline Wilson